Utah Territory

Acts, resolutions and memorials passed

And adopted during the sixteenth annual session of the Legislative

Assembly of the Territory of Utah. Published by virtue of an act approved

Jan. 18, 1867 - Vol. 10

Utah Territory

Acts, resolutions and memorials passed
*And adopted during the sixteenth annual session of the Legislative Assembly of the
Territory of Utah. Published by virtue of an act approved Jan. 18, 1867 - Vol. 10*

ISBN/EAN: 9783337810986

Printed in Europe, USA, Canada, Australia, Japan

Cover: Foto ©ninafisch / pixelio.de

More available books at **www.hansebooks.com**

RESOLUTIONS AND MEMORIALS

PASSED AND ADOPTED DURING THE

SIXTEENTH ANNUAL SESSION

OF THE

LEGISLATIVE ASSEMBLY

OF THE

TERRITORY OF UTAH.

————:o:————

PUBLISHED BY VIRTUE OF AN ACT APPROVED JAN. 18, 1867.

————:o:————

GREAT SALT LAKE CITY:
JAMES A. THOMPSON, PUBLIC PRINTER.

1867.

———:o:———

INDEX TO FORMS. APPENDIX.

ACTS,

RESOLUTIONS AND MEMORIALS

PASSED AND ADOPTED DURING THE SIXTEENTH ANNUAL SESSION
OF THE LEGISLATIVE ASSEMBLY

OF THE

TERRITORY OF UTAH.

———:o:———

CHAPTER I.

An ACT to incorporate the Alpine City Library Association

Sec. 1.—Be it enacted by the Governor and Legislative Assembly of the Territory of Utah: That Thomas J. McCulloch, John W. Vance, John Carlisle, William Strong, and William Daniels, their associates and successors in office, are hereby constituted a body corporate, to be known and styled "Alpine City Library Association;" and shall have power to purchase, receive and hold property real and personal; to sue and be sued, plead and be impleaded, defend and be defended in all courts of law and equity; and to do all things that may be proper to carry into effect the objects of the Association by establishing a library of books, maps, charts and scientific instruments, connecting therewith a reading room and lectures; and the above named persons are hereby appointed a Board of Directors of said Association, until superseded as provided in the following section.

Sec. 2.—A Board of five Directors shall be elected by the members of said Association on the second Monday in February, 1867, and biennially thereafter on said day, who shall hold their office two years, and until their successors are duly elected; and they shall have power to appoint a President, Secretary, Corresponding Secretary, Treasurer and Librarian, and define their duties; and also to make such bye-laws as may be necessary to do all business of the Association. A majority may form a quorum to do business, and may fill any vacancy in the Board until the next regular election.

Sec. 3.—This Association may raise means by sale of shares, by contributions and donations for the purchase of books, maps, charts and other furnishings and apparatus, and for leasing or erecting suitable buildings for the library, reading rooms and lectures.

Sec. 4.—Conditions of membership admission to the library, reading room and lectures, and the loaning of books or other property shall be as provided by the bye-laws of the Association.

Approved Dec. 21, 1866.

CHAPTER II.

Deficiency Bill.

Be it enacted by the Governor and Legislative Assembly of the Territory of Utah:
That the sum of eight hundred and twenty-seven dollars and eighty-two cents is
hereby appropriated, out of any money in the Territorial Treasury not otherwise appropriated, to reimburse A. P. Rockwood, Warden of the Penitentiary, for moneys
expended by him to December 1, 1866, above the amount appropriated for Penitentiary
purposes by the Legislative Assembly during its Annual Session, 1865-66.

————:o:————

CHAPTER III.

An ACT to incorporate the Moroni City Library and Literary Association.

Sec. 1.—Be it enacted by the Governor and Legislative Assembly of the Territory
of Utah: That Michael Johnson, Charles Longson, John Done, Jabez Faux, Ruel M.
Rodgers, Aaron Hardy and Charles Kemp, their associates and successors in office, are
hereby constituted a body corporate, to be known and styled Moroni City Library and
Literary Association, and shall have power to purchase, receive and hold property
real and personal; to sue and be sued, plead and be impleaded, defend and be defended
in all courts of law and equity; and to do and perform all things that may be necessary and proper to enable them to carry into effect the objects of this Association in
the diffusion of knowledge, by establishing a library of books, maps, charts and scientific instruments, connecting therewith a reading room and scientific and other popular lectures; and the above named persons are hereby appointed a Board of Directors
of said Association, until superseded as provided in the following section.
Sec. 2.—A Board of seven Directors may be elected by the members of said Association on the second Monday in February annually, who shall hold their office for
one year and until their successors are duly elected. They shall have power to appoint
a President, Secretary, Treasurer, Librarian and such other officers as may be deemed
necessary, and define their duties, and to enact such bye-laws as may be fitting for the
proper management of all business of the Association. A majority may form a quorum
to do business, and they may fill any vacancy in the Board until the next regular
election.
Sec. 3.—This Association may raise means by shares, contributions and donations
for the purchase of books, maps, charts or any other desirable thing to further the
intent of this Act; and for leasing or erecting suitable buildings for the library, reading room and lectures; and new members may be added on such conditions as may
be prescribed in the bye-laws of the Association; and the library and reading room
shall be open for the use of the public, and books loaned out under such regulations
and at such times as the Board of Directors may determine.
Approved Dec. 21, 1866.

————:o:————

CHAPTER IV.

An ACT to provide for Convening the Seventeenth and subsequent Annual Sessions of the Legislative Assembly.

Be it enacted by the Governor and Legislative Assembly of the Territory of Utah:
That the next Annual Session of the Legislative Assembly shall convene in the State
House in Great Salt Lake City; and said session shall begin at two o'clock, p.m., of
the second Monday in January, one thousand eight hundred and sixty-eight, and
annually thereafter.
Approved Jan. 8, 1867.

CHAPTER V.

An ACT incorporating the Beaver City Library Association.

Sec. 1.—Be it enacted by the Governor and Legislative Assembly of the Territory of Utah: That M. S. Shepherd, John Ashworth, William Fotheringham, Horace A. Skinner, A. M. Farnsworth, William J. Cox, Daniel Tyler and W. G. Nowers, with their associates and successors in office, are hereby constituted a body corporate, to be known and styled the Beaver City Library Association; and shall have power to purchase, receive and hold property real and personal; to sue and be sued, plead and be impleaded, defend and be defended in all courts of law and equity; and to do and perform all things that may be necessary and proper to enable them to carry into effect the objects of the Association in the diffusion of knowledge, by establishing a library of books, maps, charts and scientific instruments, connecting therewith a reading room and scientific and other popular lectures; and the above named persons are hereby appointed a Board of Directors of said Association, until superseded as provided in the following section.

Sec. 2.—A Board of seven Directors may be elected by the members of said Association on the first Monday of March, 1867, and annually thereafter on said day, who shall hold their office one year and until their successors are duly elected; and they shall have power to appoint a President, Secretary and Treasurer, Librarian and other officers as may be deemed necessary, and define their duties; and also to enact such bye-laws as may be necessary for the proper management of all business of the Association. A majority may form a quorum to do business, and they may fill any vacancy in the Board until the next regular election.

Sec. 3.—This Association may raise means by shares, contributions and donations for the purchase of books, maps, charts, &c., and for leasing or erecting suitable buildings for the library, reading room and lectures. New members may be added on such conditions as may be prescribed in the bye-laws of the Association, and the library and the reading room shall be open for the use of the public, or books may be loaned out under such regulations and at such times as the Board of Directors may determine.

Approved Jan. 10, 1867.

——:o:——

CHAPTER VI.

An ACT to provide for the election of a Delegate to the House of Representatives of the United States.

Sec. 1.—Be it enacted by the Governor and Legislative Assembly of the Territory of Utah: That an election shall be held on the first Monday of February, 1867, at the usual places of holding elections in the several counties of the Territory, for the election of a Delegate to the House of Representatives for the Fortieth Congress. The election shall be held, conducted and returns thereof made agreeable to an "Act regulating elections," "approved Jan. 3, 1853." The Delegate for the Forty-first Congress shall be elected at the general election on the first Monday of August, 1868, and biennially thereafter.

Sec. 2.—This Act shall be in force from and after the passage thereof.

Approved Jan. 10, 1867.

CHAPTER VII.

An ACT to incorporate Beaver City, in Beaver County.

Sec. 1.—Be it enacted by the Governor and Legislative Assembly of the Territory of Utah: That all that portion of country situated within the following boundaries, to wit: beginning at a point one and a half miles south of the bridge across Beaver River at the point where the military road crosses Beaver River, thence east two miles, thence north six miles, thence west six miles, thence south six miles, thence east four miles to the place of beginning, shall be known and designated by the name of Beaver City; and the inhabitants thereof are hereby constituted a body corporate and politic by the name aforesaid, and may have and use a common seal which they may change and alter at pleasure.

Sec. 2.—The inhabitants of said city, by the name and style aforesaid, shall have power to sue and be sued, to plead and be impleaded, defend and be defended in all courts of law and equity, and in all actions whatsoever; to purchase, receive and hold property real and personal in said city; to purchase, receive and hold real property beyond the city for burying grounds or other public purposes for the use of the inhabitants of said city; to improve and protect such property, and to do all other things in relation thereto as natural persons.

Sec. 3.—There shall be a City Council, to consist of a Mayor and five Councilors, who shall have the qualifications of electors of said city, and shall be chosen by the qualified voters thereof, and shall hold their offices for two years and until their successors shall be elected and qualified. The City Council shall judge of the qualifications, elections and returns of their own members, and a majority of them shall form a quorum to do business; but a smaller number may adjourn from day to day, and compel the attendance of absent members under such penalties as may be prescribed by ordinance; there shall also be elected in like manner two Justices of the Peace, who shall have the qualifications of voters, be commissioned by the Governor and have jurisdiction in all cases arising under the ordinances of the city.

Sec. 4.—The Mayor and Councilors, before entering upon the duties of their offices, shall take and subscribe an oath or affirmation that they will support the Constitution of the United States and the laws of this Territory, and that they will well and truly perform all the duties of their offices to the best of their skill and abilities.

Sec. 5.—One Mayor and five Councilors shall be elected biennially, and the first election under this Act shall be at such times in said city as the Probate Judge of Beaver County shall direct: Provided, said election shall be on or before the first Monday in August next. Said election shall be held and conducted as now is provided by law for the holding of elections for County and Territorial officers; and, at the first election, all voters shall be entitled to vote.

Sec. 6.—The clerks of election shall leave with each person elected, or at his usual place of residence, within five days after the election, a written notice of his election; and each person so notified shall, within ten days after the election, take the oath or affirmation hereinbefore mentioned, a certificate of which oath shall be deposited with the Recorder, whose appointment is hereinafter provided for, and be by him preserved; and all subsequent elections shall be held, conducted and returns thereof be made as may be provided for by ordinance of the City Council.

Sec. 7.—The City Council shall have authority to levy and collect taxes for city purposes upon all taxable property, real and personal, within the limits of the city, not exceeding one half of one per cent. per annum upon the assessed value thereof; and may enforce the payment of the same, to be provided for by ordinance not repugnant to the Constitution of the United States or to the laws of this Territory.

Sec. 8.—The City Council shall have power to appoint a Recorder, Treasurer, Assessor and Collector, Marshal and Supervisor of Streets. They shall also have the power to appoint all such other officers, by ordinance, as may be necessary, define the duties of all city officers and remove them from office at pleasure.

Sec. 9.—The City Council shall have power to require of all officers, appointed in pursuance of this Act, bonds with security, for the faithful performance of their respective duties, and also to require of all officers, appointed as aforesaid, to take an oath for the faithful performance of the duties of their respective offices.

Sec. 10.—The City Council shall have power and authority to make, ordain, establish and execute all such ordinances, not repugnant to the Constitution of the United States or the laws of this Territory, as they may deem necessary for the peace, benefit, good order, regulation, convenience and cleanliness of said city; for the protection of property therein from destruction by fire or otherwise, and for the health and happiness of the inhabitants thereof; and shall have control of the water of the Beaver River: Provided, that such control shall not be exercised to the injury of any rights already acquired by actual settlers thereon; and shall have control of the water courses and mill privileges within said city; but in no case shall they interfere with the natural rights of others heretofore acquired in relation to water. They shall have power to fill all vacancies that may happen by death, resignation or removal of any of the officers herein made elective; to fix and establish the fees of the officers of said Corporation. The City Council shall have power to divide the city into Wards and specify the boundaries thereof.

Sec. 11.—All ordinances passed by the City Council shall, within ten days after they shall have been passed, be published in some newspaper printed in said city, or certified copies thereof be posted up in three of the most public places in the city. They shall not be in force until thus published or posted up.

Sec. 12.—All ordinances of the city may be proven by the Seal of Corporation affixed thereto; and, when printed or published in book or pamphlet form, purporting to be printed or published by the authority of the Corporation, the same shall be received in evidence in all courts and places, without further proof.

Sec. 13.—The Justice of the Peace of said city shall have all the the powers of other Justices of the Peace, both in civil and criminal cases arising under the laws of the Territory. They shall perform the same duties, be governed by the same laws and give the same bonds and securities as other Justices of the Peace. They shall have exclusive jurisdiction in all cases arising under the ordinances of the Corporation, and shall issue such process as may be necessary to carry such ordinances into execution. Appeals may be had from any decision or judgment of said Justices, arising under the ordinances of said city, or the laws of the Territory, to the Probate Court of said Beaver County, in the same manner as appeals are or may be taken from other Justices of the Peace.

Sec. 14.—The Mayor shall be the Chief Executive Officer of said Corporation; he shall preside in the City Council, and shall have power to veto any ordinance when not passed by four-fifths majority, and it shall be his duty to sign all city ordinances.

Sec. 15.—This Act shall be in force on and after the tenth day of February, one thousand eight hundred and sixty-seven, and may be amended or repealed at the pleasure of the Legislative Assembly.

Approved Jan. 10, 1867.

————:o:————

CHAPTER VIII.

An ACT incorporating the Coalville Library Association.

Sec. 1.—Be it enacted by the Governor and Legislative Assembly of the Territory of Utah: That John Boyden, William H. Smith, Ira N. Hinckley, George H. Knowlden and C. L. Hawkins, of Coalville, Summit County, Utah Territory, and their successors in office, are hereby constituted a body corporate with perpetual succession, to be known and styled the Coalville Library Association; and shall have power to purchase, receive and hold property; to sue and be sued, to plead and be impleaded, defend and be defended in all courts of law and equity and in all actions whatsoever; and to do and perform all things that may of right pertain to their duties in the regulation, control and suitably providing for the interests and in carrying into effect the objects of this organization; and the above named persons are hereby appointed a Board of Directors of said Association, until an election shall take place.

Sec. 2.—That a Board of Directors shall be elected by the members of said Association on the first Monday in January, eighteen hundred and sixty-eight, and thereafter annually. The Directors shall have power to appoint a President, Secretary, Treasurer and Librarian, and such other officers as may be deemed necessary; also to fill any vacancy that may occur in the Board; and at the close of their term of office shall present to the Association a report of the number of books, papers and other publications on hand, the amount of moneys received and disbursed during the year, the number of books donated and by whom; also the amount incurred for services of Librarian and other incidental expenditures. A majority of the Directors shall constitute a quorum to do all business; and for the proper management of the library and reading room they shall have power to frame bye-laws which, upon receiving the sanction of two-thirds of the members present at any stated meeting, shall be in full force.

Sec. 3.—That the library and reading room shall be for the use and benefit of the public, subject to such regulations as may in the bye-laws be prescribed.

Sec. 4.—Conditions of membership shall be as made and provided by the Directors.

Approved Jan. 11, 1867.

————:o:————,

CHAPTER IX.

An ACT changing the County Seat of Kane County.

Be it enacted by the Governor and Legislative Assembly of the Territory of Utah: That the County Seat of Kane County is hereby removed from Grafton to Rockville in said County; and that so much of "An Act defining the boundaries of Counties and locating County Seats," "approved January 10th, 1866," as locates the County Seat at Grafton, is hereby repealed.

Approved Jan. 12, 1867.

————:o:————

CHAPTER X.

An ACT to incorporate Fillmore City, in Millard County,

Sec. 1.—Be it enacted by the Governor and Legislative Assembly of the Territory of Utah: That all that district of Millard County embraced in the following boundaries, to wit: beginning at a point three miles due east of the southeast corner of the Public Square now surveyed, thence south three miles, thence west six miles, thence north six miles, thence east six miles, thence south three miles to the place of beginning, shall be known and designated under the name and style of Fillmore City, and the inhabitants thereof are hereby constituted a body corporate and politic by the name aforesaid, and may have and use a common seal, which they may change and alter at pleasure.

Sec. 2.—The inhabitants of said city, by the name and style aforesaid, shall have power to sue and be sued, to plead and be impleaded, defend and be defended in all courts of law and equity and in all actions whatsoever; to purchase, receive and hold property real and personal; to purchase, receive and hold real property beyond the city for burying grounds or other public purposes for the use of the inhabitants of said city; to sell, lease, convey or dispose of property, real and personal, for the benefit of said city; to improve and protect such property, and to do all other things in relation thereto as natural persons.

Sec. 3.—There shall be a City Council to consist of a Mayor and five Councilors, who shall have the qualifications of electors of said city, and shall be chosen by the qualified voters thereof, and shall hold their offices for two years and until their successors shall be elected and qualified. The City Council shall judge of the qualifications, elections and returns of their own members, and a majority of them shall form a quorum to do business; but a smaller number may adjourn from day to day and compel the attendance of absent members, under such penalties as may be prescribed by ordinance; there shall also be elected in like manner two Justices of the Peace who shall have the qualifications of voters, be commissioned by the Governor, and have jurisdiction in all cases arising under the ordinances of the city.

Sec. 4.—The Mayor and Councilors, before entering upon the duties of their offices shall take and subscribe an oath or affirmation that they will support the Constitution of the United States and the laws of this Territory, and that they will well and truly perform all the duties of their offices to the best of their skill and abilities.

Sec. 5.—One Mayor and five Councilors shall be elected biennially, and the first election under this Act shall be at such time and place as the Probate Judge of Millard County shall direct: Provided, said election shall be on or before the first Monday in August next. Said election shall be held and conducted as is now provided by law for the holding of elections for County and Territorial officers; and at the said first election all electors within said city limits shall be entitled to vote.

Sec. 6.—The Clerks of election shall leave with each person elected, or at his usual place of residence, within five days after the election, a written notice of his election; and each person so notified shall, within ten days after the election, take the oath or affirmation hereinbefore mentioned, a certificate of which oath shall be deposited with the Recorder, whose appointment is hereinafter provided for, and be by him preserved; and all subsequent elections shall be held, conducted and returns thereof made as may be provided for by ordinance of the City Council.

Sec. 7.—The City Council shall have authority to levy and collect taxes, for city purposes, upon all taxable property real and personal within the limits of the city, not exceeding one half of one per cent. per annum upon the assessed value thereof; and may enforce the payment of the same in any manner, to be provided by ordinance, not repugnant to the Constitution of the United States or the laws of this Territory.

Sec. 8.—The City Council shall have power to appoint a Recorder, Treasurer, Assessor and Collector, Marshal and Supervisor of Streets. They shall also have power to appoint all such other officers, by ordinance, as may be necessary, define the duties of all city officers and remove them from office at pleasure.

Sec. 9.—The City Council shall have power to require of all officers, appointed in pursuance of this Act, bonds with security for the faithful performance of their respective duties, and also to require of all officers, appointed as 'aforesaid, to take an oath for the faithful performance of the duties of their respective offices.

Sec. 10.—The City Council shall have power and authority to make, ordain, establish and execute all such ordinances, not repugnant to the Constitution of the United States or the laws of this Territory, as they may deem necessary for the peace, benefit, good order, regulation, convenience and cleanliness of said city; for the protection of property therein from destruction by fire or otherwise, and for the health and happiness of the inhabitants thereof; and shall have control of the water and water courses leading to the city: Provided, that such control shall not be exercised to the injury of any rights already acquired by actual settlers thereon; and shall have control of the water courses and mill privileges within said city; but in no case shall they interfere with the natural rights of others acquired in relation to water privileges within said city. They shall have power to fill all vacancies that may happen by death, resignation, removal, or otherwise, in any of the offices herein made elective; to fix and establish the fees of the officers of said Corporation; to impose such fines, not exceeding one hundred dollars, and imprisonment not exceeding six months, for each offense, for the breach or violation of any city ordinance; to divide the city into Wards and specify the boundaries thereof.

Sec. 11.—All ordinances passed by the City Council shall, within one month after they they shall have been passed, be published in some newspaper printed in said city, or certified copies thereof be posted up in three of the most public places in the city.

Sec. 12.—All ordinances of the city may be proven by the Seal of the Corporation; and when printed or published in book or pamphlet form, purporting to be printed or published by the authority of the Corporation, the same shall be received in evidence in all courts and places, without further proof.

Sec. 13.—The Justices of the Peace of said city shall have all the powers of other Justices of the Peace, both in civil and criminal cases arising under the laws of the Territory; they shall perform the same duties, be governed by the same laws, give the same bonds and securities as other Justices of the Peace; they shall have exclusive jurisdiction in all cases arising under the ordinances of the Corporation, and shall issue such process as may be necessary to carry such ordinances into execution. Appeals may be had from any decision or judgment of said Justices, arising under the ordinances of said city or the laws of the Territory, to the Probate Court of Millard County, in the same manner as appeals are or may be taken from other Justices of the Peace

Sec. 14.—The Mayor shall be the Chief Executive Officer of said Corporation; he shall preside in the City Council, and shall have power to veto any ordinance when not passed by four-fifths majority; and it shall be his duty to sign all city ordinances.

Sec. 15.—The City Council shall have power to restrain, regulate or prohibit the running at large of cattle, horses, mules, sheep, swine, goats and all kinds of poultry; and to tax and regulate the keeping of dogs, and to authorize the destruction of the same when at large contrary to city ordinance.

Sec. 16.—To license, regulate, prohibit or restrain the manufacturing, selling or giving away of spirituous, vinous or fermented liquors, tavern keepers, dram or tippling shop keepers, boarding, victualing or coffee houses, restaurants, saloons or other houses or places for the selling or giving away of ardent, vinous or fermented liquors.

Sec. 17.—All ordinances, resolutions and regulations now in force in Fillmore City, and not inconsistent with this Act, shall remain in force until altered, modified or repealed by the City Council after this Act shall take effect.

Sec. 18.—This Act shall not invalidate any act done by the present City Council of Fillmore City, or by its officers, nor divest their successors, under this Act, of any right, property, or otherwise, or liability which may have accrued to or been created by said Council prior to the passage of this Act.

Sec. 19.—The City Council shall have exclusive power by ordinance to regulate the Police of the city; to license, tax and regulate auctioneers, merchants and retailers; to license, tax and regulate theatrical and other exhibitions, shows and amusements; to tax, restrain, prohibit and suppress gaming, bawdy and other disorderly houses.

Sec. 20.—This Act shall be in force on or after the tenth day of February, 1867, and may be amended or repealed at the pleasure of the Legislative Assembly.

Sec. 21.—"An Act to incorporate Fillmore City, Millard County," "approved Feb. 13, 1852," is hereby repealed.

Approved Jan. 12, 1867.

——:o:——

CHAPTER XI.

An ACT to incorporate the City of Grantsville.

Sec. 1.—Be it enacted by the Governor and Legislative Assembly of the Territory of Utah: That all that district of country embraced in the following boundaries in Tooele County, to wit: commencing two and a half miles due east from a point known as the lumber bridge situated on the county road running through Grantsville in Tooele County, thence south two miles, thence west four and a half miles, thence north four and a half miles, thence east four and a half miles, thence south two and one half miles to the place of beginning, shall be known and designated under the name and style of Grantsville City; and the inhabitants thereof are hereby constituted a body corporate and politic by the name aforesaid, and shall have perpetual succession; and may have and use a common seal, which they may change and alter at pleasure.

Sec. 2.—The inhabitants of said city, by the name and style aforesaid, shall have power to sue and be sued, to plead and be impleaded, defend and be defended in all courts of law and equity and in all actions whatsoever; to puchase, receive, hold, sell, lease, convey and dispose of property, real and personal, for the benefit of said city, both within and without its corporate boundaries; to improve and protect such property, an to do all other things in relation thereto as natural persons.

Sec. 3.—The municipal government of said city is hereby vested in a City Council to be composed of a Mayor, three Aldermen, one from each Ward, and five Councilors, who shall have the qualifications of electors of said city, and shall be chosen by the qualified voters thereof, and shall hold their office for two years and until their successors are elected and qualified.

Sec. 4.—An election shall be held on the first Monday of March next, and every two years thereafter on said day, at which there shall be elected one Mayor, three Aldermen, five councilors and one Justice of the Peace; and the persons respectively receiving the highest number of votes cast in the city for said officers shall be declared elected. When two or more candidates shall have an equal number of votes for the same office, the election shall be determined by the City Council.

Sec. 5.—The first election under this Act shall be conducted in the following manner, to wit: the County Clerk of Tooele County shall cause notice of the time and place, and the number and kind of officers to be chosen, to be posted up in four public places in said city at least ten days previous to said election. Two Judges shall be selected by the Probate Judge of Tooele County at least one week previous to the day of election. Said Judges shall choose two Clerks, and the Judges and Clerks, before entering upon their duties; shall take and subscribe an oath or affirmation, before the County Court, for the faithful performance of said duties. The polls shall be open at 8 o'clock a.m., and shall close at 6 o'clock p.m. At the close of the election the Judges shall seal up the ballot box and the list of names of the electors, and transmit the same, within two days from the time of holding such election, to the County Clerk of Tooele County. As soon as the returns are received, the County Clerk, in the presence of the Probate Judge, shall unseal and examine them, and furnish, within five days, to each person having the highest number of votes, a certificate of his election. In case of a tie, it shall be decided by lot drawn by the County Clerk in presence of the Probate Judge.

Sec. 6.—All subsequent elections held under this Act shal be held, conducted and returns thereof made as may be provided for by ordinance of the City Council.

Sec. 7.—The City Council shall be judge of the qualifications, elections and returns of their own members, and a majority of them shall form a quorum to do business, shall determine the rules of their own proceedings, and shall meet at such time and place as they may direct; and the Mayor shall preside when present, and have a casting vote; and, in the absence of the Mayor, any Alderman present may be appointed to preside over said meeting.

Sec. 8.—The City Council may hold stated meetings, and special meetings may be called by the Mayor or any two Aldermen, by notice to each of the members of said Council, served personally or left at his usual place of abode.

Sec. 9.—The City Council shall have power to appoint a Marshal, Recorder, who shall be the Auditor of Public Accounts, Treasurer, Assessor and Collector, Supervisor of Streets, Surveyor, an Attorney, a Sexton, a Sealer of Weights and Measures, and such other officers as may be necessary, define their duties, remove them from office at pleasure, and fix and establish the fees of all city officers.

Sec. 10.—All officers, elected in accordance with the fourth section of this Act, may be removed for cause from such office by a vote of two-thirds of the City Council, and shall be furnished with the charges and have an opportunity to be heard in their defence; and the Council shall have power to compel the attendance of witnesses and the production of papers when necessary.

Sec. 11.—When any vacancy shall happen by the death, resignation or removal of any officer, such vacancy may be filled by the City Council; and every person elected or appointed to any office under this Act shall, before he enters upon the duties thereof, take and subscribe an oath or affirmation that he will support the Constitution of the United States, the laws of this Territory and the ordinances of the city, and that he will well and truly perform all the duties of his office to the best of his knowledge and ability; and he shall be required to give bonds as shall be prescribed by the city ordinances, which oath and bonds shall be filed with the city Recorder.

Sec. 12.—The City Council shall have power to divide the city into Wards and specify the boundaries thereof, and, when necessary, create additional Wards, and add to the number of Aldermen and Councilors, and proportion them among the several Wards as may be just and most conducive to the welfare of said city.

Sec. 13.—The Justice of the Peace shall be a Conservator of the Peace within the limits of the city, and shall give bonds and qualify as other Justices of the Peace; and when so qualified shall possess the same powers and jurisdiction, both in civil and criminal cases arising under the laws of the Territory, and may be commissioned by the Governor as a Justice of the Peace in and for said city. He shall account for and pay over all fines and forfeitures, arising under the ordinances of the city, into the city Treasury, and all fines and forfeitures, arising under the laws of the Territory, into the County Treasury; and shall issue such process as may be necessary to carry into effect all ordinances of said city. Appeals may be had, from any decision or judgment of a Justice's Court, in the same manner as are or may be provided by statute for appeals from Justice's Courts; and he shall account for and pay over to the city Treasury, within three months, all fines or forfeitures received by him by virtue of his office; and he shall keep a docket, subject at all times to the inspection of the City Council and all other parties interested.

Sec. 14.—All process issued by the Justice of the Peace shall be directed to the Marshal or other legal officer; and, in execution thereof, he shall be governed by such rules and regulations as may be provided by city ordinance.

Sec. 15.—It shall be the duty of the Recorder to make and keep accurate records of all the ordinances made by the City Council and all their proceedings in a Corporate capacity, which record shall at all times be open to the inspection of the electors of said city and all other parties interested; and shall audit all accounts of said Incorporation. He shall have and keep a plat of all surveys within the city; and he is

B

hereby authorized to take the acknowledgment of deeds, transfers and other instruments of writing, and shall perform such other duties as may be required of him by city ordinance.

Sec. 16.—The Treasurer shall receive all money or funds belonging to the city, and shall keep an accurate account of all receipts and expenditures in such manner as the City Council shall direct. He shall pay all funds, that may come to his hands by virtue of his office, upon orders signed by the Auditor of Public Accounts; and shall report to the City Council a true account of his receipts and disbursements, as they may require.

Sec. 17.—The City Council shall have power within the city, by ordinance, to annually levy and collect taxes on the assessed value of all property in the city made taxable by the laws of the Territory, for the following named purposes, to wit: not to exceed five mills on the dollar for contingent expenses, nor to exceed five mills on the dollar to open, improve and keep in repair the streets of the city. The City Council is further empowered to divide the city into School Districts, provide for the election of Trustees, appoint a Board of School Inspectors, annually assess and collect and expend the necessary tax for school purposes, and for furnishing the city with water for irrigating and other purposes, and regulate and control the same; and furthermore, so far as may be necessary, to control the water courses leading thereto.

Sec. 18.—The City Council shall have the management and control of the finances and property of said city.

Sec. 19.—To require, and it is hereby made the duty of, every able male resident of the city, over the age of eighteen and under the age of fifty years, to labor not to exceed two days in each year upon the streets; but every person may, at his option, pay two dollars for the day he shall be so bound to labor, provided it be paid within five days from the time he shall be notified by the Street Supervisor. In default of payment as aforesaid, the same may be collected as other taxes.

Sec. 20.—The City Council shall have power to borrow money for city purposes, the interest of which shall not exceed one-fourth of the city revenue arising from taxes of the previous year.

Sec. 21.—The City Council shall have power, by ordinance, to regulate the form of the assessment rolls. The annual assessment roll shall be returned by the Assessor on or before the first Monday in June of each year, but the time may be extended or additions made thereto by order of the City Council. On the return thereof, the City Council shall fix a day for hearing objections thereto; and any person feeling aggrieved by the assessment of his property may appear at the time specified and make his objections, which shall be heard and determined upon by the City Council; and they shall have power to alter, add to, take form and otherwise correct and revise said assessment roll.

Sec. 22.—The Collector shall be furnished, within thirty days after the assessment rolls are corrected, with a list of taxes to be collected; and, if not paid when demanded, the Collector shall have power to collect said taxes with interest and cost, by suit in the Corporate name, as may be provided by ordinance. The assessment roll shall in all cases be evidence on the part of the Corporation.

Sec. 23.—To appropriate and provide for the payment of the expenses and debts of the city.

Sec. 24.—To make regulations to prevent the introduction of contagious diseases into the city; to make quarantine laws and enforce the same within the city and around it, not exceeding ten miles next beyond the boundaries thereof.

Sec. 25.—To examine, license and regulate the practice of surgeons and physicians; to prohibit, prevent and punish, by fine and imprisonment, the imposition of quacks and other medical pretenders; to establish hospitals and infirmaries, and make regulations to secure the general health of the inhabitants; to declare what shall be nuisances and prevent and remove the same.

Sec. 26.—To provide the city with water; to dig wells, lay pump logs and pipes and erect pumps in the streets for the extinguishment of fires and the convenience of the inhabitants.

Sec. 27.—To direct or prohibit the location and management of houses for the storing of gunpowder, tar, pitch, resin or other combustible and dangerous materials within the city, and to regulate the conveying of gunpowder.

Sec. 28.—To exclusively control, regulate, repair, amend and clear the streets, alleys, bridges, sidewalks or crosswalks, and open, widen, straighten or vacate streets and alleys and put drains or ditches and sewers therein, and prevent the encumbering of the streets in any manner, and protect the same from any encroachment and injury.

Sec. 29.—To provide for the lighting of the streets and erecting lamp posts; to erect market houses and establish markets and market places, and provide for the government and regulation thereof.

Sec. 30.—To provide for the erection of all needful buildings for the use of the city, and for enclosing, improving and regulating all public grounds belonging to the city.

Sec. 31.—To license, regulate, prohibit or restrain the manufacturers, sellers or venders of spirituous or fermented liquors, tavern keepers, dram or tippling-shop keepers, boarding, victualing or coffee houses, restaurants, saloons or other houses or places for the selling or giving away of wines or other liquors, whether ardent, vinous or fermented.

Sec. 32.—To license, tax and regulate auctioneers, merchants, retailers, groceries, ordinaries, hawkers, peddlers, brokers, pawnbrokers and money changers.

Sec. 33—To regulate the selling or giving away of any ardent spirits or other intoxicating liquors by any shopkeeper, grocer or trader, to be drank in any shop, store, grocery, outhouse, yard, garden or other place within the city, except by persons or at places duly licensed; to forbid the selling or giving away of ardent spirits or other intoxicating liquors to any child, apprentice or servant, without the consent of his or her parent, guardian, master or mistress, or to any Indian.

Sec. 34.—To regulate and license or prohibit butchers, and to revoke their license for malconduct in the course of trade, and to regulate, license and restrain the sale of fresh meat and vegetables in the city.

Sec. 35.—To license, tax, regulate, suppress or prohibit billiard tables, pin alleys, nine or ten pin alleys, or table and ball alleys; to suppress or restrain all disorderly houses and groceries; to authorize the destruction and demolition of instruments and devices used for the purpose of gaming, and all kinds of gambling; to prevent any riot, noise, disturbance or disorderly assemblages; and to retain and punish vagrants, mendicants, street beggars and prostitutes.

Sec. 36.—To regulate, suppress or prohibit all exhibitions of common showmen, shows of every kind, concerts or other musical entertainments, exhibitions of natural or artificial curiosities, caravans, circuses, theatrical performances, ball rooms and all other exhibitions and amusements.

Sec. 37.—To license, tax and regulate hacking, carriages, wagons, carts and drays, and fix the rates to be charged for the carriage of persons and for wagonage, cartage and drayage of property; as also to license and regulate porters and fix the rate of porterage.

Sec. 38.—To provide for the prevention and extinguishment of fires; to regulate the fixing of chimneys and flues thereof and stove pipes; and to organize and establish fire companies.

Sec. 39.—To regulate and order prrapet walls and other partition fences.

Sec. 40—To establish standard weights and measures, and regulate the weights and measures to be used in the city, in all cases not provided for by law.

Sec. 41.—To provide for the inspecting and measuring of lumber and other building materials, and for the measurement of all kinds of mechanical work.

Sec. 42.—To provide for the inspection and weighing of hay, lime and stone coal, and the measuring of charcoal, firewood and other fuel to be sold or used within the city.

Sec. 43.—To provide for and regulate the inspection of tobacco, beef, pork, flour and meal, also beer, whisky and brandy, and all other spirituous or fermented liquors.

Sec. 44.—To regulate the weight and quality of bread sold and used in the city.

Sec. 45.—The City Council shall have exclusive power within the city, by ordinance, to license, regulate or restrain the keeping of ferries and toll bridges.

Sec. 46.—To provide for taking the enumeration of the inhabitants of the city; to regulate the burial of the dead, and registration of births and deaths; to direct the returning and keeping of bills of mortality, and to impose penalties on physicians, sextons and others for any default in the premises.

Sec. 47.—To prevent horse racing, immoderate riding or driving in the streets, and to authorize their being stopped by any person; to punish or prohibit the abuse of animals; to provide for the putting up of posts in the front of city lots, to which to fasten horses and other animals; to compel the fastening of horses, mules, oxen or other animals attached to vehicles, while standing or remaining in the streets.

Sec. 48.—To prevent the encumbering of the streets or sidewalks, lanes, alleys or public grounds with carriages, tents, wagons, carts, sleighs, horses or other animals, sleds, wheelbarrows, boxes, lumber, timber, firewood, posts, awnings, signs, adobies or any material or substance whatever.

Sec. 49.—To restrain, regulate or prohibit the running at large of cattle, horses, mules, sheep, swine, goats and all kinds of poultry; and to tax, prevent or regulate the keeping of dogs, and to authorize the destruction of the same when at large contrary to city ardinance.

Sec. 50.—To compel the owner or occupant of any grocery, cellar, tallow chandler shop, soap factory, tannery, stable, barn, privy, sewer or any unwholesome place to cleanse, remove or abate the same from time to time, as often as may be necessary for the health, comfort and convenience of the inhabitants of said city

Sec. 51.—To direct the location and management of and regulate breweries and tanneries; and to direct the location, management and construction of and restrain or prohibit within the city distilleries, slaughtering establishments and all establishments or places where nauseous, offensive or unwholesome business may be carried on.

Sec. 52.—To prevent any person from bringing, depositing or having within the limits of the city any dead carcass or any unwholesome substance, and to require the removal or destruction of the same by any person who shall have placed or caused to be placed upon or near his premises or near any of the streams of this city any such substance, or any putrid or unsound beef, pork or fish, hides or skins of any kind; and, on his default, to authorize the removal or destruction of the same by any officer of said city.

Sec. 53.—To direct and regulate the planting and preserving trees in the streets and public grounds; and regulate the fencing of lots within the boundaries of the city.

Sec. 54.—To prevent the ringing of bells, the blowing of horns and bugles, the crying of goods and all other noises, performances and devices tending to disturb the peace and quiet of the city.

Sec. 55.—To grant and issue licenses, and direct the manner of issuing and registering thereof. Bonds may be taken on the granting of licenses, for the due observance of the ordinances of the City Council.

Sec. 56.—To require every merchant, retailer, trader and dealer in merchandise or property of every description, which is sold by measure or weight, to cause their weights and measures to be sealed by the City Sealer and to be subject to his inspection; the standard of which weights and measures shall be conformable to those established by law.

Sec. 57.—The City Council shall have power to make such ordinances and resolutions, not contrary to nor conflicting with the constitution and laws of the United States and the laws of this Territory, as may be necessary and expedient to carry into effect the powers vested in the City Council or any officer of said city by this Act; and enforce observance of all ordinances and resolutions made in pursuance of this Act, by penalties not exceeding one hundred dollars, or imprisonment not to exceed six months, or both.

Sec. 58.—The City Council shall have exclusive authority and power to establish and regulate the Police of the city; to impose fines, forfeitures and penalties for the breach of any ordinances; to provide for the recovery of such fines and forfeitures and the enforcement of such penalties; and to pass, make, ordain, establish and execute all such ordinances, not repugnant to the constitution and laws of the United States or the laws of this Territory, as they may deem necessary for carrying into effect and execution the powers specified in this Act, and for the peace, good order, regulation, convenience and cleanliness of the city, for the protection of property therein from destruction by fire or otherwise, and for the health, safety and happiness of the inhabitants thereof.

Sec. 59.—To provide for the punishment of offenders and vagrants by imprisonment in the county or city jail, or by compelling them to labor on the streets or other public works until the same shall be fully paid, in all cases where such offenders or vagrants shall fail or refuse to pay the fines and forfeitures which may be awarded against them.

Sec. 60.—All ordinances passed by the City Council shall, within one month after they have been passed, be published in some newspaper printed in said city, or certified copies thereof be posted up in three of the most public places in said city.

Sec. 61.—All ordinances of the city may be proven by the seal of the Corporation; and, when printed or published in book form, purporting to be printed or published by authority of the City Council, the same shall be received in evidence in all courts or places without further proof.

Sec. 62.—When it shall be necessary to take private property for opening, widening or altering any public street, lane, avenue or alley, the Corporation shall make a just compensation therefor to the person whose property is so taken; and if the amount of such compensation cannot be agreed upon, a Justice of the Peace shall cause the same to be ascertained by a jury of six disinterested men, who shall be inhabitants of the city.

Sec. 63.—All jurors, empannelled to inquire into the amount of benefit or damage that shall happen to the owners of property so proposed to be taken, shall first be sworn to that effect; and shall return to the Mayor or presiding officer of the City Council their inquest in writing, signed by each juror.

Sec. 64.—All officers of the city, created conservators of the peace by this Act, shall have power to arrest or cause to be arrested, with or without process, all persons who shall break the peace, commit for examination and, if necessary, detain such persons in custody, not exceeding forty-eight hours, in the city prison or other safe place; and shall have and exercise such other powers, as conservators of the peace, as the City Council may prescribe.

Sec. 65.—The City Council shall cause to published in some newspaper published in Grantsville City, or posted up in three public places, on or before the first day of December in each year, a statement of the amount of the city revenue, specifying in said statement whence derived and for what disbursed.

Approved Jan. 12, 1867.

---:o:---

CHAPTER XII.

An ACT incorporating Brigham City.

Sec. 1.—Be it enacted by the Governor and Legislative Assembly of the Territory of Utah: That all that district of country embraced in the following boundaries in Box Elder County, to wit: commencing at the southeast corner of Martin Luther Ensign's land claim on the Territorial road, about one mile northeast of the Court House in Brigham City, thence west to the Big Slough between said Territorial road and Bear River west, thence south along said Slough to a point west of the lane passing between the two enclosures called the Welsh Field and Welsh Settlement, thence east to the west line of Cache County, thence north to a point east of the place of beginning, and thence west to the place of beginning, shall be known and designated under the name and style of Brigham City; and the inhabitants thereof are hereby constituted a body corporate and politic by the name aforesaid, and shall have perpetual succession, and may have and use a common seal which they change and alter at pleasure.

Sec. 2.—The inhabitants of said city, by the name and style aforesaid, shall have power to sue and be sued, to plead and be impleaded, defend and be defended in all courts of law and equity, and in all actions whatsoever; to purchase, receive and hold property real and personal in said city; to purchase, receive and hold real property beyond the city for burying grounds or other public purposes for the use of the inhabitants of said city; to sell, lease, convey or dispose of property real and personal for the benefit of said city; to improve and protect such property, and to do all other things in relation thereto as natural persons.

Sec. 3.—There shall be a City Council, to consist of a Mayor and five Councilors, who shall have the qualifications of electors of said city, and shall be chosen by the qualified voters thereof, and shall hold their offices for two years and until their successors shall be elected and qualified. The City Council shall judge of the qualifications, elections and returns of their own members, and a majority of them shall form a quorum to do business; but a smaller number may adjourn from day to day, and compel the attendance of absent members under such penalties as may be prescribed by ordinance; there shall also be elected in like manner two Justices of the Peace, who shall have the qualifications of voters, be commissioned by the Governor and have jurisdiction in all cases arising under the ordinances of the city.

Sec. 4.—The Mayor and Councilors, before entering upon the duties of their offices, shall take and subscribe an oath or affirmation that they will support the Constitution of the United States and the laws of this Territory, and that they will well and truly perform all the duties of their offices to the best of their skill and abilities.

Sec. 5.—One Mayor and five Councilors shall be elected biennially, and the first election under this Act shall be at such times in said city as the Probate Judge of Box Elder County shall direct: Provided, said election shall be on or before the first Monday in August next. Said election shall be held and conducted as now is provided by law for the holding of elections for County and Territorial officers; and, at the said first election, all electors within said city limits shall be entitled to vote.

Sec. 6.—The clerks of election shall leave with each person elected, or at his usual place of residence, within five days after the election, a written notice of his election; and each person so notified shall, within ten days after the election, take the oath or affirmation hereinbefore mentioned, a certificate of which oath shall be deposited with the Recorder, whose appointment is hereinafter provided for, and be by him preserved; and all subsequent elections shall be held, conducted and returns thereof made as may be provided for by ordinance of the City Council.

Sec. 7.—The City Council shall have authority to levy and collect taxes for city purposes upon all taxable property, real and personal, within the limits of the city, not exceeding one half of one per cent. per annum upon the assessed value thereof; and may enforce the payment of the same, to be provided for by ordinance not repugnant to the Constitution of the United States or to the laws of this Territory.

Sec. 8.—The City Council shall have power to appoint a Recorder, Treasurer, Assessor and Collector, Marshal and Supervisor of Streets. They shall also have the power to appoint all such other officers, by ordinance, as may be necessary, define the duties of all city officers and remove them from office at pleasure.

Sec. 9.—The City Council shall have power to require of all officers, appointed in pursuance of this Act, bonds with security, for the faithful performance of their respective duties, and also to require of all officers, appointed as aforesaid, to take an oath for the faithful performance of the duties of their respective offices.

Sec. 10.—The City Council shall have power and authority to make, ordain, establish and execute all such ordinances, not repugnant to the Constitution of the United States or the laws of this Territory, as they may deem necessary for the peace, benefit, good order, regulation, convenience and cleanliness of said city; for the protection of property therein from destruction by fire or otherwise, and for the health and happiness of the inhabitants thereof; and shall have control of the water and water courses leading to the city: Provided, that such control shall not be exercised to the injury of any rights already acquired by actual settlers thereon; and shall have control of the water courses and mill privileges within said city; but in no case shall they interfere with the natural rights of others heretofore acquired in relation to water. They shall have power to fill all vacancies that may happen by death, resignation, removal, or otherwise, of any of the officers herein made elective; to fix and establish the fees of the officers of said Corporation. The City Council shall have power to divide the city into Wards and specify the boundaries thereof.

Sec. 11.—All ordinances passed by the City Council shall, within ten days after they shall have been passed, be published in some newspaper printed in said city, or certified copies thereof be posted up in three of the most public places in the city. They shall not be in force until thus published or posted up.

Sec. 12.—All ordinances of the city may be proven by the Seal of Corporation affixed thereto; and, when printed or published in book or pamphlet form, purporting to be printed or published by the authority of the Corporation, the same shall be received in evidence in all courts and places, without further proof.

Sec. 13.—The Justices of the Peace of said city shall have all the powers of other Justices of the Peace, both in civil and criminal cases arising under the laws of the Territory. They shall perform the same duties, be governed by the same laws and give the same bonds and securities as other Justices of the Peace. They shall have exclusive jurisdiction in all cases arising under the ordinances of the Corporation, and shall issue such process as may be necessary to carry such ordinances into execution. Appeals may be had from any decision or judgment of said Justices, arising under the ordinances of said city, or the laws of the Territory, to the Probate Court of said Box Elder County, in the same manner as appeals are or may be taken from other Justices of the Peace.

Sec. 14.—The Mayor shall be the Chief Executive Officer of said Corporation; he shall preside in the City Council, and shall have power to veto any ordinance when not passed by four-fifths majority, and it shall be his duty to sign all city ordinances.

Sec. 15.—The City Council shall have power to restrain, regulate or prohibit the running at large of cattle, horses, mules, sheep, swine, goats and all kinds of poultry; and to tax and regulate the keeping of dogs, and to authorize the destruction of the same when at large contrary to city ordinance.

Sec. 16.—To license, regulate, prohibit or restrain the manufacturing, selling or giving away of spirituous, vinous or fermented liquors, tavern keepers, dram or tippling shop keepers, boarding, victualing or coffee houses, restaurants, saloons or other houses or places for the selling or giving away of ardent, vinous or fermented liquors.

Sec. 17.—The City Council shall have exclusive power by ordinance to regulate the Police of the city; to license, tax and regulate auctioneers, merchants and retailers; to license, tax and regulate theatrical and other exhibitions, shows and amusements; to tax, restrain, prohibit and suppress gaming, bawdy and other disorderly houses.

Sec. 18.—This Act shall be in force on and after the tenth day of February, one thousand eight hundred and sixty-seven, and may be amended or repealed at the pleasure of the Legislative Assembly.

Approved Jan. 12, 1867.

CHAPTER XIII.

An ACT changing the time of holding elections in the City of Springville and extending the east boundary line of said City.

Sec. 1.—Be it eneacted by the Governor and Legislative Assembly of the Territory of Utah: That the next election for officers of said city shall be held on the first Monday in August next, 1867, and every two years thereafter.

Sec. 2.—That the corporate powers of said city shall extend over and embrace all that portion of territory described within the following boundaries, viz: beginning at the northeast corner of said City Incorporation, running thence due east to the summit of the mountains, thence in line of summit of said mountains to a point due east of the southeast corner of the said City Incorporation, thence due west to the last named corner: Provided, that all rights heretofore granted by the County Court of Utah County within said described territory shall remain in force.

Sec. 3 —Any law conflicting with this Act is hereby repealed.

Sec. 4.—This Act shall be in force from and after its passage.

Approved Jan. 14, 1867.

————:o:————

CHAPTER XIV.

An ACT authorizing the Auditor of Public Accounts to settle the accounts of Alvin Nichols, Assessor and Collector of Box Elder County, for the year 1857.

Be it enacted by the Governor and Legislative Assembly of the Territory of Utah: That the Auditor of Public Accounts is hereby authorized to settle the accounts of Alvin Nichols, Assessor and Collector of Box Elder County, for the year 1857, as the said Auditor shall deem most equitable as between the aforesaid Territory and Nichols, all the circumstances of the case considered; and such settlement shall be deemed a final adjustment of said accounts.

Approved Jan. 14, 1867.

————:o:————

CHAPTER XV.

An ACT incorporating the Provo City Library and Reading Room Association.

Sec. 1.—Be it enacted by the Governor and Legislative Assembly of the Territory of Utah: That Isaac Bullock, Leonard John Nuttall, James E. Daniels, Samuel S. Jones, Peter Stubbs, David Cluff, jr., David John and their associates and successors are hereby constituted a Body Corporate, under the name and style of the Provo City Library and Reading Room Association; and by said name shall have power to purchase, receive and hold property real and personal; to sue and be sued, plead and be impleaded, defend and be defended in all courts of law and equity; to have and use a common seal and alter the same at pleasure; to make and adopt such bye-laws as they may deem requisite and proper for carrying into effect the object of the Association, not repugnant to the Constitution of the United States or the laws of this Territory.

Sec. 2.—The object of this Association shall be to establish and conduct a library of books, maps, charts and scientific instruments, and connect therewith a lecture and reading room; and to collect and preserve evidences of the early and current history of this Territory, its progress in settlement and population; and for this purpose said Association may raise means by the sale of shares and by contribution and donation.

Sec. 3.—The members of said Association shall, on or before the first Monday in August, eighteen hundred and sixty-seven, and annually thereafter on the second Monday in February, elect a President, Secretary and five Directors, who shall hold office for one year, or until their successors are duly elected; they shall constitute a Board, a majority of whom may form a quorum to do business, and shall have power to fill all vacancies that may occur in the Board by death, or otherwise, and to appoint a Treasurer, Librarian and such other officers as may necessary to carry into effect the provisions of this Act.

Sec. 4.—The conditions of membership, admission to the library, reading room and lectures and the loaning of books or other property shall be as prescribed by the bye-laws of said Association.

Sec. 5.—This Act shall be in force from and after its passage.

Approved Jan. 15, 1867.

————:o:———

CHAPTER XVI.

An ACT incorporating the Provo Cañon Road Company.

Sec. 1.—Be it enacted by the Governor and Legislative Assembly of the Territory of Utah: That Alexander F. McDonald, Warren N. Dusenbury, and Shadrach Holdaway of Utah County, William M. Wall and Nymphas Murdock of Wasatch County, and such other persons as may become stockholders in the Corporation hereby created, are made and constituted a Body Corporate for the purposes hereinafter specified, under the name and style of the Provo Cañon Road Company, with perpetual succession for the term of twenty years; and in their corporate name shall have power to sue and be sued in all actions at law and equity in any court having jurisdiction; to purchase and hold, lease, rent or convey real estate or personal property; to sell and transfer the same, and to do and perform any and all acts in their Corporate name that any individual can or has a lawful right to do; to make and use a common seal, and to alter the same at pleasure; and to do all other acts necessary for the proper exercise of the powers conferred and the privileges granted in this Act.

Sec. 2.—The capital stock shall be fifty thousand dollars, and may be increased by said Corporators to any sum not exceeding one hundred and fifty thousand dollars, which shall be divided into shares of fifty dollars each and deemed personal property. Each subscriber of stock shall pay, at the time of subscribing, twenty per cent. of the sum subscribed, and the remainder in installments when called for by the Board of Directors. Shares shall be represented by a certificate signed by the President and Secretary, and shall be transferable upon the books of the Company in such manner as their bye-laws may direct. Shareholders shall be entitled to one vote for each share, at all elections or business meetings.

Sec. 3.—The Corporators, or a majority of them, may open books for the subscription of stock at Provo City, at such time and place as they may appoint, twenty days notice of which shall be given by posting notices in six of the most public places in Utah and Wasatch Counties; and when the sum of ten thousand dollars is subscribed, said Corporators, or a majority of them, shall give notice in like manner to the stockholders to meet and organize said Company by electing a President and five Directors, whose term of office shall be two years and until their successors are elected and qualified.

Sec. 4.—The President and Directors, before entering upon the duties of their offices to which they have been elected, shall give bonds, conditioned for the faithful performance of their duties, to the acceptance of the Probate Judge of Utah County and filed in his office. The said President and Directors shall form a Board, a majority of whom may do business, and shall have power to fill all vacancies that may occur in the Board by death, or otherwise; to appoint a Secretary, Treasurer, Superintendent of Roads and all officers necessary to carry into effect the provisions of this Act; and may require them to give bonds conditioned for the faithful performance of their duties; and shall have power to ordain and make such bye-laws and regulations as may be necessary for building, protecting and keeping in repair Provo Cañon Road; for the preservation of the timber in the Cañon and its tributaries, and for all purposes whatsoever pertaining to the interest of said Company, not contravening the laws of the United States or of this Territory.

Sec. 5.—The said Company shall have the right and privilege, and the same is hereby granted, to build a good substantial wagon road through Provo Cañon, commencing at Provo City and extending through said Cañon to Provo Valley in Wasatch County. And when the aforesaid Company shall have completed said road to the acceptance of the Territorial Road Commissioner, a toll gate may be established thereon and toll collected at the following rates:

For each vehicle drawn by two animals				$1 50
"	"	"	four "	2 00
"	"	"	six "	2 50
"	additional pair of	"		1 00
"	vehicle drawn by one animal			75
"	pack	"		15
"	horseman			15
For loose horses, mules or cattle, each				10
" sheep, goats or swine	"			5

Provided, that persons hauling timber, fuel or produce from within thirty miles of Provo City shall pay but one way, being entitled to a return ticket free.

Sec. 6.—Any person forcibly or fraudulently passing any toll gate erected on said road shall, for each offense, be liable to a fine not exceeding one hundred dollars and costs, to be prosecuted for in any court having jurisdiction, by any officer, agent, servant, or stockholder, in the name of said Company; and if any person shall obstruct, break, injure or destroy any part of the road of said Company, or any work or fixture attached to or in use upon the same, the person or persons so offending shall, for every such offense, be liable to a civil suit for the recovery of damages by said Company, and shall also be subject to indictment and, upon conviction, shall be punished by fine not exceeding five hundred dollars and imprisonment not exceeding six months, at the discretion of the court.

Sec. 7.—Any toll gatherer, duly authorized by the President and Directors of said Company, may detain and prevent from passing through his gate any person riding, leading or driving animals and any carriage or other vehicle, until he has received the tolls authorized by this Act.

Sec. 8.—Nothing in this Act shall be so construed as to prevent the Legislative Assembly from altering and amending the same at pleasure.

Sec. 9.—An Act entitled "An Act to incorporate the Provo Kanyon Road Company," "approved January 20th, 1865," is hereby repealed.

Approved Jan. 15, 1867.

————:o:————

CHAPTER XVII.

An ACT incorporating the City of Coalville, in Summit County.

Sec. 1.—Be it enacted by the Governor and Legislative Assembly of the Territory of Utah: That all that district of country embraced in the following boundaries, in Summit County, to wit: commencing at the Wasatch Coal Bed, thence south three miles, thence west to the Weber River, thence down the west bank of said river three miles, thence east to the place of beginning, shall be known and designated under the name and style of Coalville City; and the inhabitants thereof are hereby constituted a body corporate and politic by the name aforesaid, and shall have perpetual succession, and may have and use a common seal which they may change and alter at pleasure.

Sec. 2.—The inhabitants of said city, by the name and style aforesaid, shall have power to sue and be sued, to plead and be impleaded, defend and be defended in all courts of law and equity, and in all actions whatsoever; to purchase, receive and hold

c

property real and personal in said city; to purchase, receive and hold real property beyond the city for burying grounds or other public purposes for the use of the inhabitants of said city; to sell, lease, convey or dispose of property real and personal for the benefit of said city; to improve and protect such property, and to do all other things in relation thereto as natural persons.

Sec. 3.—There shall be a City Council, to consist of a Mayor and five Councilors, who shall have the qualifications of electors of said city, and shall be chosen by the qualified voters thereof, and shall hold their offices for two years and until their successors shall be elected and qualified. The City Council shall judge of the qualifications, elections and returns of their own members, and a majority of them shall form a quorum to do business; but a smaller number may adjourn from day to day, and compel the attendance of absent members under such penalties as may be prescribed by ordinance; there shall also be elected in like manner two Justices of the Peace, who shall have the qualifications of voters, be commissioned by the Governor and have jurisdiction in all cases arising under the ordinances of the city.

Sec. 4.—The Mayor and Councilors, before entering upon the duties of their offices, shall take and subscribe an oath or affirmation that they will support the Constitution of the United States and the laws of this Territory, and that they will well and truly perform the duties of their offices to the best of their skill and abilities.

Sec. 5.—One Mayor and five Councilors shall be elected biennially, and the first election under this Act shall be at such times in said city as the Probate Judge of Summit County shall direct: Provided, said election shall be on or before the first Monday in August next. Said election shall be held and conducted as now is provided by law for the holding of elections for County and Territorial officers; and, at the said first election, all electors within said city limits shall be entitled to vote.

Sec. 6.—The clerks of election shall leave with each person elected, or at his usual place of residence, within five days after the election, a written notice of his election; and each person so notified shall, within ten days after the election, take the oath or affirmation hereinbefore mentioned, a certificate of which oath shall be deposited with the Recorder, whose appointment is hereinafter provided for, and be by him preserved; and all subsequent elections shall be held, conducted and returns thereof made as may be provided for by ordinance of the City Council.

Sec. 7.—The City Council shall have authority to levy and collect taxes for city purposes upon all taxable property, real and personal, within the limits of the city, not exceeding one half of one per cent. per annum upon the assessed value thereof; and may enforce the payment of the same, to be provided for by ordinance not repugnant to the Constitution of the United States or to the laws of this Territory.

Sec. 8.—The City Council shall have power to appoint a Recorder, Treasurer, Assessor and Collector, Marshal and Supervisor of Streets. They shall also have the power to appoint all such other officers, by ordinance, as may be necessary, define the duties of all city officers and remove them from office at pleasure.

Sec. 9.—The City Council shall have power to require of all officers, appointed in pursuance of this Act, bonds with security, for the faithful performance of their respective duties, and also to require of all officers, appointed as aforesaid, to take an oath for the faithful performance of the duties of their respective offices.

Sec. 10.—The City Council shall have power and authority to make, ordain, establish and execute all such ordinances, not repugnant to the Constitution of the United States or the laws of this Territory, as they may deem necessary for the peace, benefit, good order, regulation, convenience and cleanliness of said city; for the protection of property therein from destruction by fire or otherwise, and for the benefit and happiness of the inhabitants thereof; and shall have control of the water and water courses leading to the city: Provided, that such control shall not be exercised to the injury of any rights already acquired by actual settlers; and shall have control of the water courses and mill privileges within said city; but in no case shall they interfere with the natural rights of others heretofore acquired in relation to water. They shall have power to fill all vacancies that may happen by death, resignation, removal, or otherwise, of any of the officers herein made elective; to fix and establish the fees of the officers of said Corporation. The City Council shall have power to divide the city into Wards and specify the boundaries thereof.

Sec. 11.—The City Council shall have exclusive power within the City, by ordinance, to license, regulate or restrain the keeping of ferries and toll bridges.

Sec. 12.—All ordinances passed by the City Council shall, within ten days after they shall have been passed, be published in some newspaper printed in said city, or certified copies thereof be posted up in three of the most public places in the city. They shall not be in force until thus published or posted up.

Sec. 13.—All ordinances of the city may be proven by the Seal of Corporation affixed thereto; and, when printed or published in book or pamphlet form, purporting to be printed or published by the authority of the Corporation, the same shall be received in evidence in all courts and places, without further proof.

Sec. 14.—The Justices of the Peace of said city shall have all the powers of other Justices of the Peace, both in civil and criminal cases arising under the laws of the Territory. They shall perform the same duties, be governed by the same laws and give the same bonds and securities as other Justices of the Peace. They shall have exclusive jurisdiction in all cases arising under the ordinances of the Corporation, and shall issue such process as may be necessary to carry such ordinances into execution. Appeals may be had from any decision or judgment of said Justices, arising under the ordinances of said city, or the laws of the Territory, to the Probate Court of said Summit County, in the same manner as appeals are or may be taken from other Justices of the Peace.

Sec. 15.—The Mayor shall be the Chief Executive Officer of said Corporation; he shall preside in the City Council, and shall have power to veto any ordinance when not passed by four-fifths majority, and it shall be his duty to sign all city ordinances.

Sec. 16.—The City Council shall have power to restrain, regulate or prohibit the running at large of cattle, horses, mules, sheep, swine, goats and all kinds of poultry; and to tax and regulate the keeping of dogs, and to authorize the destruction of the same when at large contrary to city ordinance.

Sec. 17.—To license, regulate, prohibit or restrain the manufacturing, selling or giving away of spirituous, vinous or fermented liquors, tavern keepers, dram or tippling shop keepers, boarding, victualing or coffee houses, restaurants, saloons or other houses or places for the selling or giving away of ardent, vinous or fermented liquors.

Sec. 18.—The City Council shall have exclusive power by ordinance to regulate the Police of the city; to license, tax and regulate auctioneers, merchants and retailers; to license, tax and regulate theatrical and other exhibitions, shows and amusements; to tax, restrain, prohibit and suppress gaming, bawdy and other disorderly houses.

Sec. 19.—This Act shall be in force on and after the tenth day of February, eighteen hundred and sixty-seven, and may be amended or repealed at the pleasure of the Legislative Assembly.

Approved Jan. 16, 1867.

———:o:———

CHAPTER XVIII.

An ACT incorporating the Kaysville Wagon Road Company.

Sec. 1.—Be it enacted by the Governor and Legislative Assembly of the Territory of Utah; That Christopher Layton, Roswell Hyde and John S. Smith, with their associates and assigns, are hereby created a Body Corporate in law, with succession for ten years, to be known by the name and style of the Kaysville Wagon Road Company; which Company shall have power to sue and be sued, to plead and be impleaded in all courts of law having jurisdiction; to receive, by gift or purchase, and hold as much real estate and personal property as may be necessary for carrying into effect the provisions or this Act; and to pass, by vote of the stockholders, all needful byelaws for the government of said Company, and may have and use a common seal which they may alter at pleasure.

Sec. 2.—The capital stock of said Company shall be ten thousand dollars, in shares of fifty dollars each, which shares shall be assignable and transferable in such manner as may be prescribed in the bye-laws of said Company.

Sec. 3.—Within thirty days next after the approval of this Act, the stockholders shall meet and proceed to organize the Company by electing the following officers:— a President, not more than five Directors, a Secretary and Treasurer, a majority of whom shall form a Board to transact the business of the Company; and they shall hold office for one year and until their successors are elected and qualified; and they shall file bonds, to the acceptance of the Territorial Treasurer, with him, conditioned for the faithful performance of their several duties. Subsequent meetings for the election of officers may be provided for in the bye-laws of said Company;

and at every election for Company officers each stockholder shall be entitled to one vote for each share of capital stock he holds, and may vote in person or by proxy.

Sec. 4.—It shall be the duty of the President and Directors of said Company to keep, or cause to be kept, in good repair the bridges and roads specified in this Act; and they shall have power to fill any vacancies which may occur in the Board of Directors by death, or otherwise, until the next election of officers; to appoint a Collector or Collectors of toll, a Superintendent of Works and such other officers and assistants as they may need; to decide the time, manner and proportions in which payments shall be made on shares, and to declare forfeited to the use of the Company the share or shares of any person who shall fail to make any payment so required to be paid, after not less than forty days notice shall have been given; and they shall cause to be issued to each stockholder a certificate of the number of shares he holds, signed by the President, countersigned by the Secretary and sealed with the seal of said Company; and no transfer of stock shall be valid in law until recorded by the Secretary of said Company.

Sec. 5.—It shall also be the duty of the Company to locate and construct, on or near the present traveled road, within one year from the approval of this Act, a good road not less than twenty feet wide; the said road to be made on the most practicable route, not to exceed one mile east of the present traveled road, to commence on the north at Kay's Creek, in Davis County, running south to Kaysville Settlement, thence along the road south to Haight's Creek in the said county; and upon the completion of one half of the distance of said road, or when evidence shall be produced to the satisfaction of the Territorial Road Commissioner that the sum of three thousand dollars shall have been justly expended upon the said road, the Company are hereby authorized and empowered to erect not exceeding one toll gate, and to demand and receive one half of the rates of toll as are hereinafter provided; and when the whole of the road shall have been completed to the acceptance of the Territorial Road Commissioner, the Company shall be entitled to demand and receive the following rates of toll, viz:

	cents
For any vehicle drawn by one or two animals	25
And for each additional pair of animals	25
For every horse or mule and rider or led horse or mule	10
" every score of neat cattle, loose horses or mules	50
" every score of sheep	25

Sec. 6.—The Secretary shall keep a record of all meetings for the transaction of business, and also keep an account of all receipts add expenditures of the Company, which at all times shall be open to the inspection of the stockholders, and be laid before the shareholders at their general meetings; and the President and Board of Directors shall make an annual report to the Legislative Assembly, during the first week of its session, of all receipts and expenditures and rates of toll; and, on or before the first day of November in each year, pay into the County Treasury ten per cent. of the nett profits of the Company arising from tolls, for the use and benefit of common schools in said county.

Sec. 7.—The Company shall keep a person constantly on duty at the gate between the hours of 6 a.m. and 9 p.m.; and from the hours of 9 p.m. to 6 a.m. travelers shall not be delayed beyond the necessary time.

Sec. 8.—The Company shall be liable for all damages to persons and property which may occur through negligence or failure on their part to comply with the conditions and specifications of this Act: Provided that, in case of floods or severe rain storms, the Company shall be allowed a reasonable time to repair damages to the road.

Sec. 9.—Any person forcibly or fraudulently passing any toll gate erected on said road shall, for each offense, be liable to a fine not exceeding one hundred dollars and costs, to be prosecuted for in any court having jurisdiction, by any officer, agent, servant or stockholder, in the name of said Company.

Sec. 10.—If any person shall obstruct, break, injure or destroy any part of the road of said Company, or any work or fixture attached to or in use by the same, the person so offending shall, for every such offense, be liable to a civil suit for the recovery of damages by said Company, and shall be subject to indictment and, upon conviction, shall be punished by fine not exceeding five hundred dollars, or imprisonment not exceeding six months, or both, at the discretion of the court.

Sec. 11.—The toll gatherer, duly authorized by the President and Directors of said Company, may detain and prevent from passing through said gate any person riding, leading or driving animals, and any carriage or other vehicle, until he has received the tolls authorized by this Act.

Sec. 12.—After the expiration of the term of ten years before mentioned in this Act, the said road shall be delivered over in good order to the Territory of Utah, to the acceptance of the Territorial Road Commissioner.

Sec. 13.—Nothing shall be so construed in this Act as to prevent the Legislative Assembly from altering and amending the same at pleasure.

Approved Jan. 16, 1867.

————:o:————

CHAPTER XIX.

An ACT incorporating the Fillmore City Library Association.

Sec. 1.—Be it enacted by the Governor and Legislative Assembly of the Territory of Utah: That Thomas R. King, Francis M. Lyman, John Kelly, Joseph V. Robinson, Hyrum Mace, Orson Holbrook and William King, their associates and successors in office, are hereby constituted a Body Corporate, to be known and styled the Fillmore City Library Association; and shall have power to purchase, receive and hold property real and personal; to sue and be sued, plead and be impleaded, defend and be defended in all courts of law and equity, and to do all other things that may be proper to carry into effect the object of this Act, by establishing a library of books, maps, charts and scientific instruments, connecting therewith a reading room and lectures; and the above named persons are hereby appointed a Board of Directors of said Association, until superseded as provided in the following section.

Sec. 2.—A Board of seven Directors shall be elected by the members of said Association on or before the first Monday in August, A. D. 1867, and biennially thereafter; said Board shall hold office two years and until their successors are elected and duly qualified, and shall have power to appoint a President, Secretary, Corresponding Secretary, Treasurer and Librarian and define their duties, and also to enact such bye-laws as may be necessary to do all the business of the Association, a majority of whom may form a quorum to do business, and may fill any vacancy in the Board until the next regular election.

Sec. 3.—This Association may raise means by the sale of shares and by contribution and donation for the purchase of books, maps, charts and scientific instruments, and for leasing or erecting suitable buildings for the library, reading rooms and lectures.

Sec. 4.—The conditions of membership, admission to the library, reading rooms, lectures and the loaning of books or other property shall be provided by the bye-laws of said Association.

Approved Jan. 16, 1867.

————:o:————

CHAPTER XX.

An ACT incorporating the Manti City Library Association.

Sec. 1.—Be it enacted by the Governor and Legislative Assembly of the Territory of Utah; That George Peacock, F. C. Roberson, John Crofford, W. K. Burton, M. D. Hamilton, E. W. Fox, L. Tuttle and John Hogard, their associates and successors in office, are hereby constituted a Body Corporate, to be known and styled Manti City Library Association; and shall have power to purchase, receive and hold property real and personal; to sue and be sued, plead and be impleaded, defend and be defended in all courts of law and equity, and to do and perform all other things that may be necessary and proper to enable them to carry into effect the objects of the Association in the diffusion of knowledge, by establishing a library of books, maps, charts and scientific instruments, connecting therewith a reading room and scientific and popular lectures; and the above named persons are hereby constituted a Board of Directors of said Association, until superseded as provided in the following section.

Sec. 2 —A Board of seven Directors shall be elected by the members of said Association on the last Saturday of February annually, who shall hold their office for one year and until their successors are duly elected; and they shall have power to appoint a President, Secretary, Treasurer, Librarian and such other officers as may be deemed necessary and define their duties, and to enact such bye-laws as may be necessary for the proper management of all business of the Association; a majority may form a quorum to do business, and they may fill any vacancy in the Board, until the next regular election.

Sec. 3.—This Association may raise means by the sale of shares and may receive contributions and donations for the purchase of books, &c., and for leasing and erecting suitable buildings for the library, reading rooms and lectures; new members may be added on such conditions as may be prescribed in the bye-laws of the Association; and the library and reading rooms shall be open for the use of the public or books loaned out under such regulations and at such times as the Board of Directors may determine.

Approved Jan. 17, 1867.

———:o:———

CHAPTER XXI.

An ACT to provide for printing and distributing the Laws and Journals of the Sixteenth Annual Session of the Legislative Assembly.

Be it enacted by the Governor and Legislative Assembly of the Territory of Utah: That the Public Printer is hereby authorized and required to print and publish in book form three thousand copies of the Acts, Resolutions and Memorials passed and adopted during this Sixteenth Annual Session of said Assembly, with index and additional legal forms and such laws and parts of laws as were accidentally omitted in printing "three thousand copies of the Digest of Laws as prepared and reported by the Joint Committee on Revision and Compilation;" and one thousand copies of the Journals in pamphlet form, including the Governor's Message and Reports of the Treasurer, Auditor, Superintendent of Schools and Directors of the Penitentiary and reports of the Directors of the Agricultural Society, together with such other documents as have been ordered spread on the Journals; and the Secretary of the Territory is hereby required to distribute the same in the manner prescribed in "An Act to provide for printing the Laws and Journals," "approved Jan. 19, 1866."

Approved Jan. 18, 1867.

———:o:———

CHAPTER XXII.

An ACT extending the boundaries of Great Salt Lake City Corporation.

Be it enacted by the Governor and Legislative Assembly of the Territory of Utah: That the boundaries of Great Salt Lake City are hereby extended as follows: commencing at the northwest corner of Great Salt Lake City Corporation limits, thence west three hundred and twenty rods, thence due south to a point opposite the southern boundary of the Corporation line of Great Salt Lake City, thence east to the River Jordan; and the boundary lines of the City Corporation of Great Salt Lake City are hereby established in accordance with the provisions of this Act.

Approved Jan. 18, 1867.

CHAPTER XXIII.

An ACT authorizing the Auditor of Public Accounts to enforce the collection of delinquent Territorial taxes, and for other purposes.

Sec. 1.—Be it enacted by the Governor and Legislative Assembly of the Territory of Utah: That the Auditor of Public Accounts is hereby authorized to enforce the collection and payment into the Territorial Treasury of all the taxes now due or that may hereafter become due the Territory, by commencing civil suits against delinquent Assessors and Collectors or ex-Assessors and Collectors on their bonds.

Sec. 2.—The County Court shall prescribe the rate per cent. for assessing and collecting Territorial and County taxes: Provided, that in no case shall more than fifteen per cent. on the amount collected be allowed for assessing and collecting.

Sec. 3.—The County Court shall, at any regular session, including the December term of the current year, hear and adjust all claims made for remittances, extenuation abatement or commutation: Provided, that after the December term of said Courts no remittance, extenuation, commutation or abatement shall be allowed by the County Courts; and the Clerks of the County Courts shall, within three months after making any alterations as aforesaid, forward a transcript thereof to the Auditor of Public Accounts, who shall file the same in his office.

Sec. 4.—The Clerks of the County Courts are hereby required to keep an accurate account of all receipts and expenditures of their respective counties, also of all debts payable to or by said counties, and annually, in the month of May, cause a true statement of the same in detail to be posted up in their offices, and keep said notices posted up during the year. A neglect of this duty by any Clerk of the County Courts shall render him liable to a fine in any sum not exceeding five hundred dollars.

Sec. 5.—A "Joint Resolution authorizing the Territorial Treasurer to collect delinquent taxes," "approved Jan. 20, 1865," is hereby repealed.

Approved Jan. 18, 1867.

————:o:———— •

CHAPTER XXIV.

Territorial Appropriation Bill.

Be it enacted by the Governor and Legislative Assembly of the Territory of Utah: That there be paid, out of any money in the Territorial Treasury not otherwise appropriated, the following amounts, viz:—

To William Clayton for services for the year 1866, as Auditor of Public Accounts,	$500 00
To said Auditor for stationery for the use of his office for 1867,	74 25
For postage, binding and printing,	48 45
To David O. Calder for services as Territorial Tresurer for 1866,	400 00
To Theodore McKeau for services as Territorial Road Commmissioner and printing for 1866,	540 00
To A. P. Rockwood for services as Warden of the Penitentiary for 1866,	1,200 00
To J. C. Rich for services as Engrossing Clerk for the Sixteenth Annual Session,	120 00
To George W. Platt for services as Engrossing Clerk for the Sixteenth Annual Session,	120 00
To be drawn on the order of R. L. Campbell, Superintendent of Common Schools, for services for the year 1866,	350 00
For traveling expenses, printing blanks and procuring educational works,	250 00
To pay the Warden for convict labor expended on the road between the paper mill and Great Salt Lake City,	649 00.
To be drawn on the order of the Recorder of Marks and Brands, for printing brand sheets for 1867,	350 00

for compensation as Deputy Attorney General to January 1, 1867, ... 400 00

To provide and furnishing books, stationery, blanks and reports and whatever may be necessary for the Adjutant General's Office, to be drawn on the order of the Lieutenant General, ... 2,000 00

To Henry McEwan, Public Printer for the Legislative Assembly of the Territory of Utah, Fifteenth Annual Session, in the years 1865-6, for printing and publishing in book form three thousand copies of the Digest of Laws as prepared by the Joint Committee on Revision and Compilation and the "Forms", ordered to be printed and published therewith, until such time as said sum is paid by the Secretary of the Territory of Utah to the aforesaid Public Printer, when it shall be by him refunded to the Territorial Treasury, ... 9,272 00

To cover the amount unappropriated, for which the Auditor has issued warrants, for Penitentiary purposes in 1865, ... 2,000 00

To amount allowed A. P. Rockwood by Act entitled "Deficiency Bill," approved, ... 827 82

To defray the expenses of the Penitentiary for 1867, ... 2,000 00

To Jesse W. Fox for services rendered as Surveyor General, ... 500 00

Amount expended over and above the appropriation made for road purposes, expended on recommendation of Territorial Road Commissioner on State roads south and west of Great Salt Lake City, ... 2,569 94

To the Territorial Road Commissioner to purchase pile driver for the Territory, ... 1,908 33

To cancel amount expended on the road in Salt Creek Cañon, in Juab County, and on the road between Manti and Gunnison, in Sanpete County, ... 103 61

To Patrick Lynch for services in assisting Secretary Reed to compile the laws, ... 300 00

For relief of Patrick Lynch as Clerk of the Third Judicial District Court, also for rent of office, &c., ... 255 00

To liquidate delinquent taxes of Richland County for 1865-6, under the direction of the County Court of Richland County, on the Territorial road leading from Huntsville to Ithaca, and that the Auditor of Public Accounts receive vouchers from said Court for said expenditure, ... 1,400 00

For the relief of Great Salt Lake County, to be drawn by J. D. T. McAllister, for the use of court and jury rooms for the Third Judicial District Court, with fuel and furniture furnished from March, 1866, to date, fifty days, at $10 00 per day, ... 500 00

For relief of J. D. T. McAllister for services as Territorial Marshal, &c., ... 665 90

To reimburse Edward Hunter and others for labor expended in widening and opening a ditch on the State road running west, immediately south of Great Salt Lake City, as petitioned for, to be drawn by and expended under the direction of the Territorial Road Commissioner, ... 500 00

To cancel amount already expended on the Territorial road from Great Salt Lake City to Wanship, in Summit County, ... 14,699 48

To improve the State road going south from Great Salt Lake City, ... 10,000 00

To partly reimburse Archibald Gardner for building a bridge across Jordan near his mill in Great Salt Lake County, ... 1,500 00

To improve the road west of Great Salt Lake City, between said city and Black Rock, ... 2,000 00

To be expended in repairing the bridge across the Weber River, also to build a bridge across the Weber River west of the present one in Weber County, and for other purposes: 5,000 90

Provided, the inhabitants of Weber County appropriate and pay an additional five thousand: Provided, also, that when Weber County shall have expended one thousand dollars, aside from the poll tax, the Territorial Road Commissioner, upon being satisfied that such amount has been laid out, shall expend one thousand dollars, and so continue until the whole ten thousand dollars be expended.

To liquidate delinquent taxes of Washington County for the years 1865-6, upon the Territorial road from St. George to Millersburg, in Washington County: 1,000 00

Provided, that when Washington County and the citzens thereof shall have expended an equal sum for the same purpose, the Auditor of Public Accounts is hereby authorized to issue orders to cancel the above amount as due from said County to the Territorial Treasury, the evidence of which shall be furnished by the Clerk of the County Court of Washington County, to the acceptance of the Territorial Road Commissioner.

All sums herein appropriated to be expended on roads and bridges shall be drawn and expended under the direction of the Territorial Road Commissioner, where other provisions have not been made.

To Franklin S. Richards for services as Clerk,..	60 00
To be drawn on the order of J. F. Smith, to pay Assistant Engrossing Clerk during the last three days of the Session,......................................	20 00
To the Perpetual Emigrating Fund for freight on set of standard weights and measures,...	478 00
To defray the expenses of forwarding specimens of the vegetable and mineral productions and manufactures of Utah Territory to the approaching Exhibition at Paris,..	1,000 00
For the relief, in part, of Gen. W. S. Snow,..	300 00
Delinquent taxes of Washington and Kane Counties, to be expended on the road from South Ash Creek coal bed by Tokerville to Kane County:...	1,500 00

Provided, the citizens of said Counties expend a like amount; said expenditures to be made under the direction of John Nebeker, Road Commissioner for Washington County.

To be drawn by the Adjutant General, to liquidate the bill of N. S. Ransohoff & Co., for merchandise furnished the Sanpete Military Expedition,...	94 00

Approved Jan. 18, 1867.

————:0:————

CHAPTER XXV.

An ACT granting to Henry S. Alexander the right to establish a toll bridge or bridges across the Weber River in Summit County.

Sec. 1.—Be it enacted by the Governor and Legislative Assembly of the Territory of Utah: That Henry S. Alexander is hereby authorized and required to erect a good substantial bridge or bridges across the Weber River, in Summit County, at or near Wanship, or where the old traveled road crosses said river; and he shall keep the same in good repair, and may take toll not to exceed the following rates, viz:

For each vehicle drawn by two animals,......................................					$1 00
"	"	"	four	"	1 50
"	"	"	six	"	2 00
"	"	"	one animal..................................		75
"	each pack		"		25
"	"	horseman,..			25
"	"	loose horse, mule, jack, camel, ox, cow, or bull,...........			10
"	"	score of sheep, goats, or swine,..........................			50

The foregoing rates shall be kept posted up at each end of the bridge during the season of taking toll; and if the said Henry S. Alexander shall fail to post up the rates of toll as required, or shall collect above the rates specified, he shall be liable to a fine not exceeding one hundred dollars for each offense: Provided, that persons hauling fuel and timber shall pay but one way, being entitled to a return ticket free.

Sec. 2.—After the completion of said bridge or bridges, if any person shall take toll upon any bridge or ferry within one mile up said river from Wanship, or within five miles down the channel of said river, he shall forfeit and pay to the party injured the sum of three thousand dollars annually, so long as said bridge or ferry shall be used.

Sec. 3.—The said Henry S. Alexander, before receiving toll as herein provided, shall execute sufficient bonds, to be approved by the Probate Judge of Summit County and filed in his office, in the sum of six thousand dollars, conditioned for the indemnifying all persons against losses they may sustain by reason of the insufficiency and unsafe condition of said bridge or bridges while toll is being received thereon, to be recovered as in action of debt before any court having jurisdiction.

Sec. 4.—The said Henry S. Alexander, at the expiration of eight years from the

D

passage of this Act, shall transfer said bridge or bridges in good condition to the Territorial Road Commissioner, as the property of the Territory.

Sec. 5.—The said Henry S. Alexander is hereby required to make an annual report, during the first week of the Legislative Assembly, of all receipts of toll received on said bridge or bridges, and pay into the Territorial Treasury, for the benefit of common schools, five per cent. of all tolls collected thereon.

Sec. 6.—Nothing in this Act shall be so construed as to prevent the Legislative Assembly from altering or amending the same at pleasure.

Approved Jan. 18, 1867.

———::———

CHAPTER XXVI.

An ACT amending "An Act granting to Alvin Nichols and William S. Godbe the right to establish a toll bridge across Bear River, in Box Elder County, and a bridge across the Malad."

Be it enacted by the Governor and Legislative Assembly of the Territory of Utah: That the word "one" is hereby changed to three, in the second line of the second section of "An Act granting to Alvin Nichols and William S. Godbe the right to establish a toll bridge across Bear River, in Box Elder County, and a bridge across the Malad," "approved Jan. 13, 1866."

Approved Jan. 18, 1867.

———:0:———

CHAPTER XXVII.

An ACT granting to Edmund Ellsworth, Sen., the right to establish a toll bridge across Weber River near Plain City, in Weber County.

Sec. 1.—Be it enacted by the Governor and Legislative Assembly of the Territory of Utah: That Edmund Ellsworth, Sen., is hereby authorized to erect a good and substantial bridge across Weber River near Plain City, in Weber County, and shall keep the same in good repair; and may take toll thereon during five years, at the following rates:

For each vehicle drawn by two animals,			$1 00
" every two additional	"		50
" " horse, or mule, rode or led,			25
" " loose animal of horse or cattle kind,			10
" " sheep, goat, or swine,			05

The foregoing rates shall be kept posted up at each end of the bridge during the season of taking toll; and if the said Ellsworth shall fail to post up the rates of toll as required, or shall collect above the rates specified, he shall be liable to a fine not exceeding one hundred dollars for each offense.

Sec. 2.—The said Ellsworth, before receiving toll as herein provided, shall execute sufficient bonds, to be approved by the Probate Judge of Weber County and filed in his office, in the sum of two thousand dollars, conditioned for indemnifying all persons against all losses they may sustain by reason of the insufficiency and unsafe condition of said bridge while toll is being received thereon, to be recovered as in an action of debt before any court having jurisdiction.

Sec. 3—Said Ellsworth is hereby required to make an annual report to the Legislative Assembly, during the first week of its session, of all tolls received on said bridge, and pay into the Territorial Treasury, for the benefit of Common Schools, five per cent. of all toll collected thereon, and turn the said bridge over to the Territorial Road Commissioner, at the expiration of the five years, in good repair.

Approved Jan. 18, 1867.

————:o:————

CHAPTER XXVIII.

An ACT to amend "an Act relating to County Recorders and the acknowledgment of Instruments of writing.

Be it enacted by the Governor and Legislative Assembly of the Territory of Utah: That section five of "An Act in relation to County Recorders and the acknowledgment of instruments of writing," "approved Jan. 19, 1855," be amended to read: Two years shall be allowed, to persons having land surveyed, to enclose the same; and in all cases where labor is expended upon dams, canals, embankments, aqueducts, or otherwise, for the purpose of irrigating said land, amounting to the sum of five dollars per acre, it shall entitle the holder of said certificate of survey to lawful possession: Provided, that where companies or associations for irrigation purposes are formed or may hereafter be formed for the improvement of lands, individuals composing said companies or associations shall not loose any right by such associations, but shall be entitled to equal privileges, in the provisions of this Act, with individual enterprise; said title shall not be invalidated or nullified, whether said lands be enclosed with fence or not.

Approved Jan. 18, 1867.

————:o:————

CHAPTER XXIX.

An ACT to incorporate the Deseret Telegraph Company.

Sec. 1.—Be it enacted by the Governor and Legislative Assembly of the Territory of Utah: That Brigham Young, Edward Hunter, A. M. Musser, E. D. Woolley, A. H. Raleigh and John Sharp of Great Salt Lake County, William Miller of Utah County, John W. Hess of Davis County, A. J. Moffatt of Sanpete County, Robert Gardner of Washington County, and such other persons as are or may become stockholders in this Corporation, are hereby created, made and constituted a Body Corporate, for the purposes hereinafter specified, under the name and style of the Deseret Telegraph Company, with perpetual succession for the term of fifty years; and in their Corporate name shall have power to sue and be sued in all actions at law and equity in any court having competent jurisdiction; to purchase and hold, lease, rent, or convey real estate or personal property; to sell and transfer the same; and to do and perform any and all other acts in their Corporate name that any individual can or has a lawful right to do; to make and use a common seal and to alter the same at pleasure; and to do all other acts necessary for the proper exercise of the powers conferred and the regulation of the privileges granted in this Act.

Sec. 2.—The capital stock shall be five hundred thousand dollars, and may be increased by said Corporators to any sum not exceeding one million dollars, and shall be divided into shares of one hundred dollars each, and be deemed personal property. Each subscriber of stock shall pay, at the time of subscribing, twenty-five per cent. of the sum subscribed, and the remainder in installments when called for by the

Board of said Corporation; the Corporators, or a majority of them, may open books for the subscription of stock, at Great Salt Lake City, at such time and place as they may appoint, by giving twenty days notice thereof in some newspaper published in said city; and when the sum of one hundred thousand dollars is subscribed, the said Corporators, or a majority of them, shall give notice of the time and place, in like manner, to the stockholders to meet and organize said Company, by electing a President, Vice-President, Secretary and Treasurer and nine Directors, who shall hold office for the term of two years and until their successors are elected and qualified; a majority of whom shall form a quorum to do business, and shall have power to fill all vacancies that may occur by death, or otherwise; said officers, before entering upon their duties, shall give bonds with approved security, conditioned for the faithful performance of their duties, to the acceptance of the Probate Judge of Great Salt Lake County, and to be filed in his office; said Board shall have power to appoint a Superintendent of Telegraph lines and such other officers as they may deem necessary, and may require them to give bonds conditioned for the faithful performance of their duties; and shall have power to ordain and make all necessary bye-laws and regulations for carrying into effect the provisions of this Act for building, protecting and keeping in repair their telegraph lines, and for all other purposes pertaining to the interest of said Company, not conflicting with the laws of the United States or of this Territory.

Sec. 3.—Each shareholder shall be entitled to a vote for each share, at all meetings of business requiring a vote, and at all general and special elections: Provided always, that absentees shall have the right to vote by proxy. Certificates of stock shall be issued by the Directors of the Company to those who have paid for shares, and shall be signed by the Treasurer and countersigned by the Secretary; said certificates may be transferred by registering the transfer on the Company's books, otherwise no transfer of stock shall be valid.

Sec. 4.—The aforesaid Company shall have the right and privilege, and the same is hereby granted, to build and construct telegraph lines to any and all parts of this Territory, and shall have power to purchase, take, receive, hold, use and rent to others to be used any patent or patents for telegraphing, and any or all rights thereunder; to purchase, take, receive, hold and maintain any and all rights, privileges and franchises relating to the business of telegraphing; to make, receive by assignment, or ratify by contract or agreement for the building, maintaining, controlling or working of any telegraph line or lines; to construct, purchase, lease, take, receive, hold, control and work any lines within the Territory of Utah, and purchase, take, lease, hold, own, use and occupy any personal or real estate, rights, property of telegraph lines, grants, franchises and privileges that may be proper and convenient for the complete transaction of its business, or for effectually and conveniently carrying out the objects and purposes of said Company; it shall also have the power to appoint such Directors, Officers and Agents and to make such rules, regulations and bye-laws as may be necessary or proper in the transaction of its business, not inconsistent with the laws of this Territory or of the United States.

Sec. 5.—The said Company is hereby authorized to construct telegraph lines along or upon any road or highway or across any of the waters or over any lands within the limits of this Territory, by the erection of the necessary fixtures, including posts, piers, or abutments, and the appropriation of any standing trees, except fruit and ornamental trees or trees within enclosures, for sustaining the wires of said lines: Provided, the same shall not be so constructed as to incommode the public use of said roads or highways, or interrupt the navigation of said waters: And provided further, that any person over whose lands said line shall pass, upon which posts, piers or abutments shall be placed, or standing trees appropriated, who shall consider himself aggrieved or damaged thereby, may, within six months after the erection of such line, make application to the Probate Court of the county in which damage is so sustained; and it shall be the duty of the said Court, on such application, to cause a notice to be served on the President or any Director of said Company; and to appoint three discreet and disinterested persons as commissioners, who shall severally take an oath, before any person authorized to administer oaths, to faithfully, impartially and justly appraise the damage sustained by said applicant by reason of said lines, piers, or abutments, or appropriation of trees, duplicates of which shall be made in writing and be signed by said commissioners, or a majority of them, one copy of which shall be given to the applicant and the other to the President or to the Director on whom the notice was served; and in case any damage shall be adjudged, the Company shall pay the amount thereof with the costs of said appraisal; said costs to be approved by the Probate Court.

Sec. 6.—Nothing in this Act shall be so construed as to prevent the Legislative Assembly from altering or amending the same at pleasure.

Approved Jan. 18, 1867.

CHAPTER XXX.

An ACT further defining the duties of the Sealer of Weights and Measures.

Sec. 1.—Be it enacted by the Governor and Legislative Assembly of the Territory of Utah: That it shall be the duty of the Sealer of Weights and Measures to procure a house or suitable room for the use of the standard weights and measures belonging to this Territory, and he shall keep open the house or room one day in each week, or as often as he may find necessary.

Sec. 2.—The Sealer of Weights and Measures shall keep an accurate account of all official receipts and disbursements, and make a report to the Legislative Assembly during the first week in each annual session.

Sec. 3.—He shall take charge of the standard weights and measures belonging to the Territory, and safely keep and preserve them until his successor is elected and qualified, to whom he shall turn them over.

Sec. 4.—The fees for sealing weights and measures shall be as follows: For each examination, testing, sealing and certifying as required from the owner of the same, viz: for any steelyards, beam, ground, floor, platform, counter or other scales by which may be weighed not exceeding one hundred pounds, seventy-five cents. For any such instrument by which may be weighed over one hundred and less than six hundred pounds, one dollar; over six hundred pounds, one dollar and fifty cents. For any nests or set of measures, seventy-five cents. For any yard stick, dry or liquor measure, twenty-five cents; and the weights attached to any scales shall, as to the compensation of the Sealer of Weights and Measures, be considered as part of the scales: Provided, that where any such weights, measures or instruments, upon subsequent examination, be found correct and shall not require to be stamped a second time, the aforesaid Sealer of Weights and Measures shall not receive more than one half the compensation provided for.

Sec. 5.—The Sealer of Weights and Measures shall examine and test any of the before mentioned instruments for weighing or measuring, on application by any person who shall tender to him the fee which, by the preceding section, he is authorized to receive; and he shall, in every case where he may employ labor or material in making accurate any weights or measures, be entitled to extra compensation therefor, and to retain the article upon which such labor or material has been employed until such compensation be paid.

Approved Jan. 18, 1867.

——:o:——

CHAPTER XXXI.

An ACT to amend "An Act defining the Judicial Districts for the Territory of Utah, prescribing the times and places of holding the Supreme and District Courts, and assigning the Chief Justice and the two Associate Justices," "approved Dec, 27, 1865."

Be it enacted by the Governor and Legislative Assembly of the Territory of Utah: That the words "second" and "November," in the second line of the second section of the Act to which this is amendatory, are hereby made to read first and October.

Approved Jan. 18, 1867.

CHAPTER XXXII.

An ACT incorporating the Deseret Irrigation and Navigation Canal Company.

Sec. 1.—Be it enacted by the Governor and Legislative Assembly of the Territory of Utah: That Brigham Young, Heber C. Kimball, Edward Hunter, Abraham O. Smoot, Robert T. Burton, Theodore McKean, Elijah F. Sheets, Reuben Miller, David Brinton, Andrew Cahoon, Isaac M. Stewart and John Sharp, with their associates, successors and assigns, are hereby created a Body Corporate in law, with perpetual succession for the term of ninety-nine years, for the purposes hereinafter specified, under the name and style of the Deseret Irrigation and Navigation Canal Company, by which name and style they shall be known; and they shall have power to sue and be sued, plead and be impleaded in all actions at law and in equity in any court having jurisdiction; to contract and be contracted with, and to purchase and to hold all necessary real estate and personal property, or to sell and transfer the same, and to do and perform all other acts in a Corporate capacity that any individual has a right to do; to make and use a common seal and alter the same at pleasure, and to do all other acts necessary for the proper exercise of the powers and the regulation of the privileges granted in this Act.

Sec. 2.—The objects of said Corporation are hereby declared to be the construction of suitable canals for the irrigation of the land lying below their level, and to afford additional water to town lots and other improved lands, and to open navigable communication from Utah Lake by way of Great Salt Lake City, and estimated to reclaim seventeen thousand acres of desert.

Sec. 3.—The capital stock of said Company shall be five hundred thousand dollars, which may, if necessary, be increased to any sum not exceeding one million two hundred thousand dollars, which capital shall be divided into shares of one hundred dollars each, and deemed personal property; and any of the afore-mentioned persons are hereby authorized to open books and receive subscriptions to this end, until the Company shall be organized.

Sec. 4.—The officers of said Company shall consist of a President, who shall preside at the Board and Company meetings, a Vice President, who shall preside in the absence of the President, and not less than five and not more than thirteen Directors, a majority of whom may form a Board to transact the business of the Company; and said Board shall appoint a Secretary and Treasurer and such other officers as they may deem necessary to carry into effect the provisions of this Act, and may require them to give bonds to the acceptance of the Board of Directors, which bonds shall be deposited at such place as the Board of Directors shall determine, and to fill all vacancies in the Board until the next general election of officers, and to pass all needful bye-laws not repugnant to the laws of the United States or of this Territory; to regulate the subscriptions for and transfers of stock; to employ workmen, and to direct the amount of compensation to be allowed to the officers, agents and employees of the Company; and, in case of the absence of the President and Vice President from any of the Board meetings, the members of the Board present may elect a President pro tem. from among their number. The President shall have power to call Board and Company meetings, or, in his absence, the Vice President may call said meetings; and, in the absence or disability of the President and Vice President, any three Directors may call a meeting of the Board or Company.

Sec. 5.—The President of the Board of Directors shall declare all dividends arising from the business of said Company, and shall make a biennial report to the Legislature of all receipts and disbursements. The Secretary shall keep an accurate account of all receipts of the Company arising from the sale of shares or of water for irrigation, rent of water power for mills or ornamental purposes, canal tolls, or otherwise, and report the same to the stockholders at least once a year; to declare all allotments or transfers of shares; to issue to each shareholder a certificate of the number of shares he holds, which certificate shall be signed by the President or Treasurer and countersigned by the Secretary and sealed with the seal of the Company; and to keep a record of the meetings of the Board and of all general meetings of the Company, and to publish all bye-laws and orders, of a public nature, made by the President and Board of Directors.

Sec. 6.—So soon as one hundred thousand dollars shall have been subscribed, the persons mentioned in the first section of this Act shall call a meeting of the stockholders; and the Company shall organize by electing a President, Vice President and Directors, who shall continue in office four years, or during the pleasure of the stockholders, the first election to be conducted by ballot; the person having the highest number of votes shall be declared elected. The manner of all elections thereafter may be prescribed in the bye-laws of the Company: Provided, that at every election for officers each stockholder shall be entitled to one vote for every share of his capital stock, and may vote in person or by proxy.

Sec. 7.—The President, Vice President and Directors shall give bonds, conditioned for the faithful performance of their duties, in the sum of five thousand dollars each, with approved security to the acceptance of Great Salt Lake County Court, which bonds shall be made payable to any person who may be injured, and shall be filed in the office of the Clerk of said Court.

Sec. 8.—The aforesaid Company is hereby authorized to construct a dam or dams across the Jordan River, to hold the water of said Lake at any height that a majority of the Selectmen of Great Salt Lake and Utah Counties may agree upon; the time and place of meeting of said Selectmen shall be appointed by the President of the Company, and their decision shall be final; and the Company shall have the right to take out on the east side of the River Jordan not to to exceed one half of the waters of said River, at any point selected by them for their dam or dams.

Sec. 9.—They shall have the power to locate a canal or canals from the said dam or dams, on the most feasible route to a point they may select in Great Salt Lake City, for irrigation, navigation, machinery, the construction of fountains, and for any useful and ornamental purpose whatever; to make, excavate and construct said canal or canals; to locate or construct basins, docks, reservoirs, aqueducts, locks, sluice-ways, weirs, dams, waste-gates, sidewalks, tow-paths, fords and bridges; to have free access to and control the same; to make, excavate and accomplish any work or device that shall be necessary for the full completion of said canal or canals, or that shall be advantageous or requisite for the efficient carrying on of navigation and irrigation, for the propelling of machinery, for the construction of fountains, or for any useful or ornamental purpose whatever; to sell, lease and dispose of the same or any portion thereof for all or any of the above purposes, on such terms and conditions as the parties may agree, and to regulate the rates of toll for navigation, and collect the same.

Sec. 10.—The main canal, when completed, shall be not less than twenty feet wide at the bottom and three feet deep; the aqueducts to be at least sixteen feet wide: Provided, that around and near the point of Utah Mountain said canal may, at first, be constructed twelve feet wide. After any canal shall have been laid out under the provisions of this Act, the Board of Directors, or any agents of theirs appointed for that purpose, may agree, with the owners of land through which it will pass, for the purchase of the right of possession of so much thereof as may be necessary for the making of the canal and the appurtenances thereunto belonging.

Sec. 11.—In every case where the owner of land so required shall be absent from the country, or from any cause shall not be capable in law so to agree, or shall refuse to agree, or ask an exorbitant price, the value of the possession of such land and the damages to the owner thereof shall be ascertained in the following manner: First.—The occupant or claimant to such land and the Board of Directors may each select a referee, and, in case of disagreement, they two may select a third; and these referees shall proceed to determine the value of the possession of the land under controversy, and assess the amount of damages, if any, which each occupant of land and owner of improvement has sustained or will sustain in consequence thereof. Second.—The appraisal, with the description of the land so appraised, shall be acknowledged by the referees signing it before the Clerk of the County Court in which the lands or improvements are situated; and, when so acknowledged, shall be filed in the County Clerk's office within ten days after it shall have been made.

Sec. 12.—The aforesaid Company, upon payment to the rightful claimant of any sum so appraised, or upon a tender thereof when the same shall be refused, shall be entitled to enter upon the possession of the lands described in the appraisal, and have and hold the same for the use and benefit of said Company forever; and if on any parcel of the lands so described there shall be no person living authorized to receive payment for the damages assessed for such parcel, and such damages shall not have been lawfully demanded within ten days after the filing of such appraisal, the Company may enter thereon without payment or tender of such damages, but subject to such payment whenever the same shall be thereafter lawfully required.

Sec. 13.—The Company shall construct good and sufficient aqueducts to conduct the waters of the canal or canals over the various streams crossed along their routes, or make such other provisions as will prevent the waters of said streams from being absorbed by the canal or canals to the injury of any person having a right in said waters.

Sec. 14.—Said Company shall make good and sufficient crossings for the accommodation of travel on all public roads crossed by said canal or canals, and shall be responsible to all parties injured through their neglect.

Sec. 15.—The Company shall furnish water, to the extent of its ability, to agriculturists along the line at uniform rates pro rata for the quantity used, the distance brought and the time it is required. No mill or other machinery that may be established shall claim or hold the water so as to prevent the irrigation of agricultural lands. The Company shall be entitled to charge such rates and tolls as will yield a fair compensation, above all necessary expenses, for the capital invested in the work, and no more. The Legislature reserves the right to modify excessive charges for the use of water or the rates of toll, and to take such action thereon as the public good may require.

Approved Jan. 18, 1867.

————:o:————

CHAPTER XXXIII.

An ACT to amend "An Act establishing a Territorial road from Great Salt Lake City to Wanship, Summit County."

Sec. 1.—Be it enacted by the Governor and Legislative Assembly of the Territory of Utah: That section three of "An Act establishing a Territorial road from Great Salt Lake City to Wanship, Summit County," is hereby so amended as to authorize the demanding and receiving not to exceed double the rates of toll hitherto authorized in said section three.

Sec. 2.—The toll collected as herein authorized shall be expended, under the direction of the Territorial Road Commissioner, in making, repairing and other incidental expenses of said road.

Sec. 3.—So much of an Act, to which this is amendatory, as conflicts with this Act is hereby repealed.

Approved Jan. 18, 1867.

————:o:————

CHAPTER XXXIV.

An ACT concerning Executions.

Sec. 1.—Be it enacted by the Governor and Legislative Assembly of the Territory of Utah: That, when an execution is issued upon a judgment or decree rendered by any court of record of this Territory, for the payment of money, it shall be the duty of the Marshal, Sheriff, or other legal officer, to whom it is directed, to levy execution on and sell the unexempted personal property of the person therein named; and in default of sufficient unexempted personal property whereon to levy to make said money, then to levy upon the unexempted land claims and improvements thereon to make the balance thereof: Provided, that in all cases the homestead occupied by the defendant and his family, including the land and improvements and appurtenances thereunto belonging, is hereby exempted from execution.

Sec. 2.—Before the officer shall sell any personal property, except by consent of parties, he shall give not less than fifteen days notice of the time, place, and kind of property to be sold, by posting up notices in not less than three of the most public places in the vicinity, and, if requested by either party, by publishing said notice in some newspaper, in general circulation, for the same length of time.

Sec. 3.—Before any land or improvement on land shall be sold on execution, it shall be the duty of the officer to cause the same to be appraised by three judicious, disinterested land holders of the vicinity, sworn to make a faithful appraisal, which oath the officer is hereby authorized to administer; and said land claims or improvements shall not be sold, unless a bid therefor is at least three-fifths of the appraised value.

Sec. 4.—Should the land claims and improvements thereon, appraised as aforesaid, be twice offered for sale and remain unsold for the want of bidders, the court issuing the execution may set the appraisal aside and order a new appraisal to be made.

Sec. 5.—It shall be the duty of the officer, having such writ, to give notice of the time and place of sale of such land claims and improvements, at least thirty days prior to such sale, in the same manner that notice is to be given in case of the sale of personal property; but the sale shall be made either on the premises or at the door of the Court House in the county where such land is situated.

Sec. 6.—If any land claim or improvement thereon shall be sold, it may be redeemed at any time within two years from the day of the confirmation of the sale by the court, by paying to the owner of the land the amount for which it sold, with interest at the rate of ten per cent. per annum, which may be paid by the debtor, or, in case of his death, by his widow, if there be one, or by his heirs, or by any of them.

Sec. 7.—It shall be the duty of the officer, selling land claims or improvements on land, to report his doings thereon to the court issuing the execution or order of sale; and, on motion of any party in interest, the court shall examine and approve the same, and order the officer to make a deed therefor, or set the same aside and order a resale, as the law and justice may require.

Sec. 8.—It shall be the duty of the officer to make a deed pursuant to the order of the court, which shall refer to the judgment or decree, the issuing the execution, the levy, sale and confirmation of sale; and such deed shall transfer all the right, title, interest and claim of the judgment debtor, to the land claim or improvement thereon, which he had at any time between the date of levy, or judgment, as the case may be, and the date of the last appraisal, if more than one has been made.

Sec. 9.—Executions issued by Justices of the Peace and Mayors and Aldermen of cities shall not be levied on land claims or improvements on land; but if any execution issued by either of them shall be returned unsatisfied in whole or in part, the judgment creditor or his agent or attorney may, if such he believes to be the fact, make affidavit that the judgment debtor has land claims or improvements on land liable to levy snd sale on execution, and file said affidavit with the Justice of the Peace, Mayor, or Alderman; and thereafter the judgment creditor may obtain a transcript of the judgment and proceedings, and file it in the Probate Court of the county in which the judgment was ordered, upon which a *scire facias* may issue; and upon return being made, "duly served," the Probate Court may award an execution to be levied on such land claims or improvements on land.

Sec 10.—Judgments and decrees for the payment of money, entered in any court of record of this Territory, shall be a lien on the land claims and improvements on land of the debtor, within the jurisdiction of the court, for two years from and after the date of such judgment or decree. Any judgment or decree for the payment of moneys, upon which an execution is not issued during any period of two years, shall become dormant, but it may be revived by *scire facias.*

Sec. 11.—Executions shall be returned to the court issuing them, on or before the following periods from their date:

When the amount of money to be made, including costs, does not exceed one hundred dollars, in fifty days.

When the amount exceeds, including costs, one hundred dollars and does not exceed five hundred dollars, ninety days.

When the amount, including costs, exceeds five hundred dollars, one hundred and twenty days.

Sec. 12.—If the purchaser, at a judicial sale of land claims or improvements on land, shall receive rents and profits from the same, or shall make valuable improvements thereon, and the same shall be redeemed as hereinbefore provided, either party may file a bill in chancery, setting forth the facts, and the court may make such order, judgment, or decree, concerning such rents, profits and improvements, as right and justice may direct.

Sec. 13.—All laws and parts of laws conflicting with this Act are hereby repealed.
Approved Jan. 18, 1867.

CHAPTER XXXV.

RESOLUTION.

Resolved by the Governor and Legislative Assembly of the Territory of Utah: That the Council and House of Representatives each be authorized to employ an Engrossing Clerk.

Approved Dec. 18, 1866.

————:o:————

CHAPTER XXXVI.

RESOLUTION authorizing the Territorial Road Commissoner to alter the Territorial road in Utah County.

Be it resolved by the Governor and Legislative Assembly of the Territory of Utah: That the Territorial Road Commissioner is hereby authorized to examine that portion of the Territorial road passing through Pleasant Grove precinct, in Utah County, and make such alterations in its location as he may deem expedient.

Approved Jan. 11, 1867.

————:o:————

CHAPTER XXXVII.

RESOLUTION concerning an appropriation for building a road over the mountain between Sevier and Piute Counties.

Be it resolved by the Governor and Legislative Assembly of the Territory of Utah: That the Territorial Road Commissioner is authorized to expend the one thousand dollars that was appropriated to be expended in making a road over the mountain between Sevier and Piute Counties, "approved Jan. 19, 1866," in assisting to build a bridge across Sevier River, between Richfield and Glenwood, in Sevier County.

Approved Jan. 12, 1867.

————:o:————

CHAPTER XXXVIII.

RESOLUTION authorizing a Committee on a Code of Practice.

Be it resolved by the Governor and Legislative Assembly of the Territory of Utah: That the President of the Council is hereby authorized to appoint a Committee of one, whose duty it shall be to take such steps as his judgment may dictate in relation to a Code of Practice for the Courts of the Territory of Utah, and report his doings thereon to the Legislative Assembly aforesaid, during the first week of its next Annual Session in 1868.

Approved Jan? 14, 1867.

——:o:——

CHAPTER XXXIX.

RESOLUTION for securing a Public Watering Place.

Be it resolved by the Governor and Legislative Assembly of the Territory of Utah: That the Territorial Road Commissioner is hereby authorized and required to examine the route of the Territorial road from Dry Creek to the point of the mountain beyond the Warm Springs in the south part of Great Salt Lake County, and locate said road at the aforesaid Springs, so as to secure them or a portion of them for a watering place for the traveling public, and to make any other alteration in the location of said road, between the aforesaid points, that he may deem expedient.

Approved Jan. 16, 1867

——:o:——

CHAPTER XL.

A RESOLUTION [extending the right to the Weber Cañon Road Company to make a wagon road from the mouth of Lost Creek to the mouth of Echo Cañon.

Be it resolved by the Governor and Legislative Assembly of the Territory of Utah: That the charter of the Weber Cañon Road Company is hereby extended for said Company to make a wagon road from the mouth of Lost Creek, in Morgan County, to the mouth of Echo Cañon, in Summit County; and that all the powers and privileges to make, keep in repair, protect and control said road, as set forth in the Weber Cañon Road Charter, are hereby conferred on said Company for the purposes herein named. Said Company shall have the right to erect a toll gate on the east end of the road not less than one mile below the mouth of Echo Cañon, and take toll thereat at the same rates as provided for taking tolls at the gates on the Weber Cañon Road.

Approved Jan. 18, 1867.

——:o:——

CHAPTER XLI.

RESOLUTION appointing a Military Code Commission.

Be it resolved by the Governor and Legislative Assembly of the Territory of Utah: That Lieutenant General Daniel H. Wells, Hon. George A. Smith and Generals

Robert T. Burton and Wm. B. Pace are hereby appointed Commissioners, whose duty it shall be to draft a Military Code of laws and regulations for the government of the militia of Utah, and report the same to the Legislative Assembly of this Territory, during the first week of its next ression, for their action thereon. •

Approved Jan. 18, 1867.

——:o:——

CHAPTER XLII.

RESOLUTION appointing a Commissioner to the Great International Exhibition at Paris.

Whereas, a great international Exhibition is to be held in Paris, France, during the approaching summer, and

Whereas, the Government of France has assigned a place in said Exhibition building for the display of products and manufactures of the United States, and invited our Government to participate in said Exhibition, by forwarding suitable specimens, and

Whereas, the necessary steps have been taken by the Federal Government to avail itself of this opportunity to make such a representation at this Great Fair of the world as will comport with the greatness of our country and give a just idea of the wonderful productiveness and resources of the land we inhabit, and

Whereas, all of the States and Territories of the Union have been invited to contribute to this international representation, and

Whereas, it is but right and proper that our mountain Territory, so remote from the great centres of population and commerce, and so recently settled under such unique circumstances, with its variety of products and manufactures, should be represented;

Therefore, be it resolved by the Governor and Legislative Assembly of the Territory of Utah: That General Brigham Young, Jun., be and is hereby appointed as Commissioner to select cereals, fruits and vegetables; also wool, cotton and flax in their raw condition, and home manufactured specimens of woolen, cotton and linen cloth; also specimens of the various minerals of the Territory and, so far as practicable, of the skins and furs of the wild animals of this region, and of every other article that will be likely to give a correct idea of the mineral and agricultural resources of this Territory and of the triumphs which have, in the brief space of nineteen years, been achieved by man, through unremitting industry and stubborn toil, over the wilderness of nature in its most forbidding form; and the said General Brigham Young, Jun., is hereby authorized to collect these various specimens, and, in his capacity as Commissioner, proceed with them to the Exhibition at Paris, France, there to display them as the products of the Territory of Utah.

Approved Jan. 18, 1867.

——:o:——

CHAPTER XLII.

MEMORIAL to Congress for an appropriation to repair the Utah Penitentiary.

To the Honorable the Senate and House of Representatives of the United States in Congress assembled:

Gentlemen:—Your Memorialists, the Governor and Legislative Assembly of the

Territory of Utah, do represent that the Utah Penitentiary is in a very poor condition, and is unfit for the safe keeping of convicts found guilty of crimes in said Territory.

Therefore, we, your Memorialists, earnestly ask your Honorable Body to appropriate twenty thousand dollars to repair the aforesaid Penitentiary, and, as in duty bound, will ever pray.

Approved Jan. 17, 1867.

————:o:————

CHAPTER XLIV.

MEMORIAL to Congress for a donation of Town Sites in aid of a Common School Fund.

To the Honorable the Senate and House of Representatives of the United States in Congress assembled:

Your Memorialists, the Governor and Legislative Assembly of the Territory of Utah, respectfully pray your Honorable Body to donate to this Territory the lands included in the recorded plots of the several Cities, Towns and Villages of this Territory, to aid in laying the foundation for a Common School Fund for the benefit of the Territory and future State; said lands to be disposed of under such regulations as the Legislature may provide.

Approved Jan. 17, 1867.

————:o:————

CHAPTER XLV.

MEMORIAL to Congress for additional Clerks in the Legislative Assembly

To the Honorable the Senate and House of Representatives of the United States in Congress assembled:

Gentlemen:—Your Memorialists, the Governor and Legislative Assembly of the Territory of Utah, would respectfully represent to your Honorable Body, that the increasing population of this Territory renders an increase of business in the Legislative Assembly unavoidable; and, considering the shortness of the session, only forty days, your Memorialists would respectfully ask your Honorable Body to enact that four additional Clerks be provided for the use of this Body, and also provide for their payment:—One Engrossing Clerk and one Enrolling Clerk for each Branch of the Assembly; and, as in duty bound, your Memorialists will ever pray.

Approved Jan. 18, 1867.

CHAPTER XLVI.

MEMORIAL to Congress for the repeal of so much of an Act as subjects all mailable matter between Kansas and California to letter postage.

To the Honorable the Senate and House of Representatives of the United States of America in Congress assembled:

Gentlemen:—Your Memorialists, the Governor and Legislative Assembly of the Territory of Utah, beg leave to state that, according to the fourth section of an Act entitled "An Act to provide for carrying the mails from the United States to foreign ports, and for other purposes," "approved March 25, 1864," all mailable matter conveyed by mail westward, beyond the western bounds of Kansas and eastward from the eastern boundary of California is subjected to letter postage, amounting almost to a prohibitory tariff upon the means and sources of information and knowledge. By this said Act your Memorialists consider that the great interior, that most needs a liberal provision for obtaining books, pamphlets, maps and charts, &c., is the only portion of country that is made to feel the prohibitory provisions of said. law, and, in the absence of more appropriate language, your Memorialists will here adopt the remarks of his Excellency Governor Durkee, in his latte annual Message to the Legislative Assembly:

"It might be well for you to call the attention of Congress to the present law requiring the prepayment of letter postage upon all mail matter, other than newspapers sent direct from the office of publication, which makes a most unjust and oppressive discrimination against the people of this and the adjoining States and Territories.

The circulation of magazines and other periodicals and the purchase of books to be forwarded by mail are virtually suspended by this law. It is a well nigh prohibitory tax upon knowledge. In our isolated condition, and with our population in many localities so sparse that good schools cannot be maintained, it is an added hardship that the dissemination of knowledge by means of books and periodicals should thus be practically denied by Congressional enactments.

You should certainly embrace in your Memorial a petition for the repeal of this oppressive law, to the end that the people of this and adjoining Territories, in respect to postal facilities, be placed upon an equality with those in the Atlantic States."

Your Memorialists would, therefore, most respectfully ask your Honorable Body to repeal the objectionable and unequal provision of this law, and thus open a door for the admission of the means of knowledge, of science and improvement as widely as it is open to other sections of country; and your Memorialists, as in duty bound, will ever pray.

Approved Jan, 18, 1867.

———:o:———

[THE FOLLOWING ACTS WERE ACCIDENTALLY LEFT OUT BY THE REVISION COMMITTEE OF 1865-6:]

An ACT to amend "An Act to incorporate Great Salt Lake City," "approved Jan. 20, 1860."

Sec. 1.—Be it enacted by the Governor and Legislative Assembly of the Territory of Utah: That appeals shall be allowed from the Mayor and Alderman's Courts of said city to the Probate Court of Great Salt Lake County, under the same regulations and restrictions as are or may be provided for appeals from Justices of the Peace to the Probate Court.

Approved Jan. 10, 1862.

An ACT to incorporate the Weber Cañon Road Company.

Sec. 1.—Be it enacted by the Governor and Legislative Assembly of the Territory of Utah: That William H. Hooper, Horace S. Eldredge, Ben Holliday of New York, Lorin Farr, Charles S. Peterson, Ira N. Spaulding, Willard Smith, and Chauncey W. West, and their associates and successors are hereby constituted a Body Corporate to be known by the name and style of Weber Cañon Road Company, for the purpose of making a Wagon road from the mouth of Weber Cañon, in Weber County, to Lost Creek settlement in Morgan County; said road to be built on the north side of Weber River; and by said name and style they and their successors shall have power from and after the passage of this Act, for the term of thirty years, to contract and be contracted with, sue and be sued in all actions at law and in equity in any court having competent jurisdiction; to do and perform any and all other acts in their Corporate name that any individual can have or has a lawful right to do; to make and use a common seal and alter the same at pleasure, and do all other acts necessary for the proper exercise of the powers and privileges conferred and granted in this Act.

Sec. 2.—The aforesaid Company shall have the right and privilege, and the same are hereby conferred, to build a good wagon road twenty feet wide, except in such places where it is not practicable, up the aforesaid Cañon to the acceptance of the Territoral Road Commissioner, and take toll thereon; and said Company shall have the right to erect two toll gates in said road at such places as they may deem best, and shall have a right to take toll at each gate at the following rates;

For every vehicle, drawn by one or two animals, not to exceed one dollar.
For every two additional animals, fifty cents.
For every horse or mule rode or led, not to exceed twenty-five cents.
For all loose animals of horse, mule or cattle kind, ten cents per head.
For sheep, goats or swine, five cents per head: Provided, all persons traveling with teams on said road, who shall return within ten days, shall have a return ticket free.

Sec. 3.—Any person wishing to become a stockholder in the aforesaid Company shall have the privilege, by paying into said Company fifty dollars; and each stockhalder shall be entitled to a vote for each share he may hold in said Company.

Sec. 4.—The officers of said Company shall consist of President, Vice President and five Directors who shall constitute a Board, a majority of whom shall form a quorum to do business and fill all vacancies that may occur in said Board by death or otherwise. The Board, before entering on the duties of their office, shall give bonds with approved security to the acceptance of a Probate Judge of Weber County, and said bond shall be filed in the office of the County Clerk. The Board of Directors are hereby empowered to appoint a Secretary, Treasurer, Superintendent of Road and all other officers that they may deem necessary, and may require them to give bonds conditioned for the faithful performance of their duties; and shall have power to ordain and make all necessary bye-laws and regulations for the carrying into effect the provisions of this Act, and for the building and keeping in repair said road, and for all other purposes whatsoever, pertaining to the interests of said Company: Provided, they make no law conflicting with the Conftitution and laws of the United States and the laws of this Territory.

Sec. 5.—Each toll gatherer, duly authorized by the President and Directors of said Company, may detain and prevent from passing through his gate any person riding, leading or driving animals, and any carriage or other vehicle, until he has received the tolls authorized by the Company.

Sec. 6.—The Director shall cause to be issued to each stockholder a certificate for the number of shares he may hold, signed by the President, countersigned by the Secretary and sealed with the seal of the Company, and no transfer of stock will be deemed valid in law, until recorded by the Secretary of said Company.

Sec. 7.—It shall be the duty of the Board of said Company to make an annual report to the Legislative Assembly, during the first week of each session, of all receipts and expenditures and rates of toll, and to pay into the Territorial Treasury, for the use and benefit of common schools, five per cent. upon the nett profits of all toll collected.

Sec. 8.—If any person or persons shall obstruct, break, injure or destroy any part of the road of said Company, or any work or fixture attached to or in use upon the road, or shall forcibly or fraudulently pass any toll gate erected on said road he shall, for every such offense, be liable to a civil suit for the recovery of damages by said Company, and may be fined in any sum not exceeding five hundred dollars for each offense, or imprisonment not to exceed six months, or both, at the discretion of the court.

Sec. 6.—It is hereby made the duty of the Probate Judge of Morgan County, directly after the publication of this Act, to open a book in which to receive subscriptions for stock in said Company; and when it shall appear that ten thousand dollars have been subscribed, he shall forthwith order an election to be held at the county seat of Morgan County for the election of a President, Vice President and five Directors for said ·Company, by publishing a notification thereof in the DESERET NEWS, setting forth the time and place of said election, in three consecutive numbers. Said election shall be held and conducted in such manner as the aforesaid Judge may direct. The persons receiving the highest number of votes for office, as contemplated in this Act, shall be declared duly elected by said Judge, who shall furnish the parties thus elected a certificate of their election. All subsequent elections shall be held at such time and place, and conducted in such manner as the Board may direct.

Sec. 10.—Nothing in this Act shall be so construed as to prevent the Legislative Assembly from altering or amending the same when they think the public good require it.

Approved Jan. 20, 1865.

FORMS.

————:o:————

1.—*Form of a Warrant.*

The Territory of Utah,   County, ss.

To any constable of said county, greeting:

Whereas complaint has been made before me, one of the justices of the peace, in and for the county aforesaid, upon the oath of E. F., that A. B., late of the county aforesaid, did, on or about the   at the county of   [here state the crime or offence, as set forth in the affidavit.]   These are therefore to command you to take the said A. B., if he [or she] be found in your county; or if he [or she] shall have fled, that you pursue after the said A. B., into any other county within this Territory, and take and safely keep the said A. B., so that you have his [or her] body forthwith, before me, or some other justice of the peace, to answer the said complaint, and be further dealt with according to law.

Given under my hand and seal, this   day of

O———— P————,   [L. S.]

————:o:————

2.—*Form of the return of a Warrant.*

I took the body of the within named A. B., and have him before the justice.

J———— W————, Constable.

Fees.

————::————

3.—*Form of a Commitment for want of Bail in Cases Bailable by Law.*

The Territory of Utah,   County, ss.

To the keeper of the jail of the county aforesaid, greeting.

Whereas, A. B., late of said county, has been arrested on the oath of E. F., [here describe the crime or offence,] and has been examined by me, O. P., one of the justices of the peace in and for said county, on such charge, and required to give bail, in the sum of   dollars for his appearance before the court of   of said county, on the first day of the next term thereof, [or forthwith, as the fact was,] which requisition he has failed to comply with; therefore, in the name of the Territory of Utah, I command you to receive the said A. B. into your custody, in the jail of the county aforesaid, there to remain until he shall be discharged by due course of law.

Given under my hand and seal, this   day of

O—— P——, [L. S.]

The above form may be used in all cases except for a capital offense (that is, for murder in the first degree), where the proof is evident, or the presumption great. In such cases the following form may be used:

3.—*Form of Commitment in Capital Cases where the proof is evident or the presumption great.*

The Territory of Utah,   county, ss.

To the keeper of the jail of the county aforesaid, greeting:

Whereas A. B., late of said county, has been arrested on the oath of E. F., for purposely and of his deliberate and premeditated malice killing and murdering one M. N. by [here set out briefly the manner of committing the crime, as by shooting the said M. N. or other means, stating it according to the fact,] on or about the day of   in the year A. D. 18—, at the county of   aforesaid, and has been examined by me, O. P., one of the justices of the peace in and for said county on such charge, and has been ordered, adjudged, and required by me to be safely kept and confined in the jail of said county, so that his body be had before the Court of of said county on the first day of the term thereof next to be holden, and from day to day, to answer such charge, the proof thereof being evident; Therefore in the name of the Territory of Utah I command you to receive the said A. B. into your custody in the jail of the county aforesaid, there to remain until he be discharged or dealt with by due course of law.

Given under my hand and seal this   day of   A. D. 18—.

O. P. [L. S.]

————:o:————

4.—*Form of Mittimus issued upon a plea of guilty and sentenced to Imprisonment in Cases of Minor Offenses.*

The Territory of Utah,   county, ss.

To the keeper of the jail of said county, greeting:

Whereas A. B. of the county aforesaid has been arrested upon the oath [or affirmation] of E. F. for [here describe the offense], and has been brought before me, O. P., one of the justices of the peace for said county, to answer said complaint, and has been admitted by me to plead guilty to said charge, and whereas the said A. B. has this day plead guilty to said charge before me and thereupon been ordered, adjudged, and sentenced by me to pay a fine to the Territory of Utah in the sum of   dollars, and to be imprisoned in the cell of the jail of said county and to be fed on bread and water only, for the term of   days, therefore in the name of the Territory of Utah I command you to receive the said A. B. into your custody, in the cell of the jail of the county aforesaid, there to be kept, confined, and imprisoned in the manner aforesaid for the said term of   days.

Given under my hand and seal this   day of   A. D. 18—, at the county aforesaid.

O. P. [L. S.]

5.—*Form of Commitment, pending a Trial.*

The Territory of Utah,   county, ss.

To the keeper of the jail of the county aforesaid, greeting:

Whereas, A. B., of the county aforesaid, has been arrested on the oath [or affirmation] of E. K. [here state the crime or offense according to the fact], and has been brought before me, O. P., one of the justices of the peace in and for said county, for trial, which trial has been necessarily postponed by reason of the [here state the absence of a material witness, or other cause of delay, according to the fact;] therefore, I command you, in the name of the Territory, to receive the said A. B. into your custody, in the jail of the county aforesaid, there to remain until discharged by due course of law.

Given under my hand and seal, this   day of   A. D. 18—.

                      O. P.   [L. S.]

———:0:———

6.—*Order for the Detention of the Prisoner in a place other than the Jail of the County, upon adjournment of the Trial.*

The Territory of Utah,   County, ss.

To J. W., constable in and for said county:

Whereas the within named A. B. has been brought before me, according to the command of this writ, and whereas the trial of the said A. B., upon the within charge, has been necessarily postponed by reason of the absence of S. H., a material witness, you are therefore hereby ordered by me to detain the said A. B. in your custody, in the dwelling house of A. Y., in said county, so that you have his body before me at my office on the   day of   , at   o'clock   M., to answer said charge, and be dealt with according to law.

Given under my hand and seal this   day of   , A. D., 18   , at said county.

           O. P., Justice of the Peace.   [L. S.]

———:0:———

7.—*Form of Mittimus after trial upon a Complaint to keep the peace.*

The Territory of Utah,   County, ss.

To the keeper of the jail of the county aforesaid, greeting:

Whereas complaint has been made before me, one of the justices of the peace within and for said county, upon the oath or affirmation of E. F., that A. B. late of said county [here set forth the substance of the charge with the allegation of fear as contained in the affidavit] and whereas I examined into the truth of said complaint, and was of opinion that there was just cause therefor, and thereupon ordered the said A. B. to enter into recognizance with security as the law directs, conditioned for the appearance of the said A. B. before the   of said county on the first day of the term thereof next to be holden, to answer said complaint, and in the meantime to keep the peace and be of good behavior—which requisition he has failed to comply with;

therefore, in the name of the Territory of Utah, I command you to receive the said A. B. into your custody in the jail of the county aforesaid, there to remain until discharged by due course of law.

Given under my hand and seal, this   day of   , A. D. 18

O. P., J. P. [L. S.]

————:0:————

8.—*Form for the return of a Mittimus.*

August   th, 18 . I committed the within named A. B. to the custody of the within named jailor, with whom I left a certified copy of this writ.

J. W., Constable.

————:0:————

9.—*Form of recognizance of the party accused, for his appearance at Court.*

The Territory of Utah,   County, ss.

Be it remembered, that on the   day of   , in the year   , A. B. and E. F. personally appeared before me, O. P., one of the Justices of the peace in and for the county aforesaid, and jointly and severally acknowledged themselves to owe the Territory of Utah the sum of   dollars, to be levied of their goods and chattels, lands and tenements, if default be made in the condition following, to wit: The condition of this recognizance is such, that if the above bound A. B. shall personally be and appear before† the Court   on the first day of the term thereof, next to be holden in and for the county aforesaid, [or if such recognizance be taken in term time, then it shall require the party to appear forthwith before such court], then and there to answer a charge of* [here name the crime or offense with which the party is charged,]and abide the judgment of the court, and not depart without leave, then this recognizance shall be void; otherwise, it shall be and remain in full force and virtue in law. Taken and acknowledged before me, on the day and year first above written.

O. P., Justice of the Peace.

————:0:————

10.—*Form of recognizance of the party accused for his appearance at court, when the case is a complaint to keep the peace.*

[Follow the last form to the star, and then set forth the particular acts of the defendant that are alleged in the affidavit as the ground or cause of the fear, and proceed thus:] and thereby causing the said M. N. to fear, and to have reason to fear, that he, the said A. B., would and was about to [here set out the acts that were feared or apprehended] and abide the order of the court thereon, and in the mean time to keep the peace and be of good behavior towards the citizens of the Territory generally, and especially towards the said M. N., then this recognizance shall be void, otherwise to be and remain in full force and virtue in law.

Taken and acknowledged before me on the day and year first above written.

O. P. Justice of the Peace.

———:o:———

11.—*Form of recognizance on adjournment of trial.*

[Follow the last form but one to the † and then proceed thus:] me at my office in the county aforesaid, on the   day of   , in the year 18—, at   o'clock P.M. of said day, then and there to answer a charge upon the oath [or affirmation] of E. F., of [here name the crime or offense] and abide my order thereon, and not depart without leave, then this recognizance shall be void; otherwise it shall be and remain in full force and virtue in law.

Taken and acknowledged before me, on the day and year first above written.

O. P. Justice of the Peace.

———:o:———

12.—*Form of Forfeiture of a Recognizance*

August 15, 1856. The within named A. B. failed to appear at any time as he was bound to do by the conditions of this his recognizance and the same became and was forfeited.   O. P. Justice of the Peace.

This forfeiture should be written on the back of the recognizance, and a minute made of it upon the docket. The recognizance and transcript should then be returned to the court, except in cases under the liquor law of 1854. Swan's St. 898.

———:o:———

13.—*Form for the Recognizance of Witnesses.*

The Territory of Utah,   county, ss.

Be it remembered that on the   day of   , in the year 18—, M. S., H. N. and A. Y., personally appeared before me, O. P., one of the justices of the peace in and for the county aforesaid, and severally acknowledged themselves to owe the Territory of Utah the sum of one hundred dollars, to be levied of their goods and chattels, lands and tenements, if default be made in the condition following, to wit:

The condition of this recognizance is such, that if the above bound M. S., H. N., and A. Y., shall personally be and appear before the   , on the first day of the term thereof, next to be holden in and for the county aforesaid, then and there to give evidence and the truth to say, on behalf of the Territory, touching such matters as shall then and there be inquired of them, and not depart the court without leave, then, and as to such of the above bound as perform this condition, this recognizance shall be void; otherwise it shall be and remain in full force and virtue in law.

Taken and acknowledged before me, on the day and year first above written.

O. P., Justice of the Peace.

———:o:———

14.—*Form of a Subpoena, for Witness.*

The Territory of Utah,   county, ss.

To any Constable of said county, greeting:

You are hereby commanded to summon M. S., H. N., and A. Y., to be and appear before me, O. P., one of the justices of the peace in and for said county, at forthwith, and there to give testimony and the truth to say, touching a certain complaint made on behalf of the Territory, against   and hereof fail not, under the penalty of one hundred dollars, and have you then and there this writ.

Given under my hand and seal, this   day of

O. P. [L. S.]

———:o:———

15.—*Form of a precept for obtaining the Defendant from Jail.*

The Territory of Utah,   County, ss.

To any Constable of the county aforesaid, greeting:

Whereas, A. B. has committed to the jail of said county, on account of the adjournment of his trial, until the   day of   A. D. 18   at 2 o'clock, P.M., upon a charge of [here set forth the offense.[You are therefore hereby commanded to receive the said A. B., from the keeper of the jail of said county, into your custody, so that you have his body before me, O. P., one of the justices of the peace of said county, at the time aforesaid, to answer said charge.

Given under my hand and seal, this   day of   A. D. 18

O. P. [L. S.]

———:o:———

16.—*Form of Affidavit to procure a Peace Warrant.*

The Territory of Utah,   County, ss.

Before me, O. P., one of the justices of the peace in and for said county, personally came, M. N., who being duly sworn according to law, deposeth and saith, that, on or about the   day of   in the year of our Lord one thousand eight hundred and   , one A. B. did [here set forth the particular acts which the defendant has done, or the words spoken, (that induce the prosecutor to fear him, and stating the time of each of such acts, as near as convenient, if more than one has occurred;] by reason of which said several acts and sayings, the said M. N. has reason to fear, and does fear that the said A. B. will [here set forth the particular wrongs or violence that the complainant is afraid will be committed by the defendant;[and further this deponent saith not.

M. N.

Sworn to and subscribed before me, at the county aforesaid, this   day of A. D. 18

O. P., Justice of the Peace.

————:o:————

17.—*Form of Docket Entry when Defendant Pleads Guilty and is Sentenced by the Justice or Mayor.*

The Territory of Utah, }
      vs.   } Petit Larceny.
A.——— B———. }

August 12, 1856. This day came E. F., and made oath, [or affirmation,] that A. B., on or about the first day of August, A. D. 1856, at the county of   . and Territory of Utah, did [here set forth the charge as set forth in the affidavit, but not copying the conclusion, or signing,] took his affidavit thereof, thereupon issued a warrant for the body of the said A. B., and delivered the same, to J. W., constable.

Same day warrant returned, with the body of the said A. B., indorsed, "I have the body of the within named A. B. Fees: service, .25, mileage, .15.

J. W., Constable."

And the said A. B. being brought before me to answer said charge, was admitted by me to plead guilty thereto; and thereupon the said A. B., for plea says that he is guilty as charged in said affidavit; whereupon the said A. B. is ordered, adjudged and sentenced by me to be imprisoned in the cell of the jail of said county and be fed on bread and water only, for the term of   days, to pay a fine to the Territory of Utah in the sum of   dollars, to pay the costs of this prosecution, taxed at   dollars [and if it be a case of larceny, then say,] and to make restitution to the said M. N., in the sum of   dollars, being double the damage of the said A. B., by reason of said theft.

Issued a Mittimus for the commitment of the said A. B. to the jail of the county for said term of   days, and delivered the same to J. W., Constable.

August 14, 1856, Mittimus returned, [here copy the return, with the items of fees;]

September 10, 1856, Execution returned, [here copy the return, with the items of fees.

————:o:————

18.— *Writ of Replevin.*

The people of the Territory of Utah, to the sheriff of the county of   greeting:

Whereas J. T., the plaintiff in this suit, complains that J. H., the defendant in this suit, hath taken and doth unjustly detain the goods, ["beasts if any"] and chattels, [if for detaining only, then these words, "hath unjustly detained and still detains" the goods [beasts] and chattels of the said plaintiff, that is to say: one wagon, two horses, &c. [here specify every item of property to be replevied:] Therefore we com-maud you, that if the said plaintiff shall give you security, as required by law, to prosecute his said complaint, and to return the aforesaid goods and chattels if a return thereof shall be adjudged, and to pay all such sums of money as may be recovered against him, thereupon, that you cause the said goods and chattels to be replevied and delivered to the said plaintiff without delay; and also that you summon the said defendant to appear before [the court, giving its proper title] at, &c., on, &c., [time and place of return] to answer the said plaintiff in the premises. And in case you cannot find the aforsaid goods and chattels, within your county, so as to replevy the same, as you are above commanded, then we do further command you, that you take the body of the said defendant, and that you have him before the said justices, [or "judges"] at the place, and on the day above mentioned, to answer the said plaintiff in the premises. And have you then there this writ, with your doings hereon.

Witness, S. N.

                                                              Clerks.

    Attty. for the Pl'ff.

————:o:————

19.—Affidavit subjoined thereto.

Territory of Utah, } ss.

J. T., [or some other person for him,] being duly sworn, doth depose and say, that he, the said plaintiff in the writ above named (and hereto annexed) is owner [or, "is now justly entitled to the possession"] of the property described in the said writ above set forth; and that the said property has not been taken for any tax, assessment, or fine, levied by virtue of any law of this Territory, nor seized under any execution or attachment against the goods and chattels of the said plaintiff liable to execution, and further this deponent saith not.

Sworn before me, &c.   J. T.

————:o:————

20.—Summons in replevin.

John Doe, }
  vs.
Richard Roe. }

By virtue of a writ of replevin to me directed and delivered, I do hereby summon you to appear before, &c., [style of the court,] at, &c., on, &c., [time and place of return of writ,] to answer John Doe, the plaintiff above named, for taking and unjustly detaining [or "for unjustly detaining,"] the following goods [beasts] and chattels, [insert the property as specified in the writ,] which said writ is prosecuted out of the said court by A. B., esquire, attorney for the said plaintiff. Dated, &c.

To Richard Roe, the above named defendant.

www.ingramcontent.com/pod-product-compliance
Lightning Source LLC
Chambersburg PA
CBHW030722110426
42739CB00030B/1187